Talking Words

Talking Words

New Essays on the Work of David Dabydeen

EDITED BY

LYNNE MACEDO

University of the West Indies Press
Jamaica • Barbados • Trinidad and Tobago

University of the West Indies Press
7A Gibraltar Hall Road   Mona
Kingston 7   Jamaica
www.uwipress.com

© 2011 by Lynne Macedo

All rights reserved. Published 2011

A catalogue record of this book is available
from the National Library of Jamaica.

ISBN: 978-976-640-257-0

Cover photograph of David Dabydeen
courtesy of the University of Warwick.

Book and cover design by Robert Harris.
Set in Adobe Garamond 11/14.5 x 27
Printed in the United States of America.

Contents

Introduction　vii
LYNNE MACEDO

Part 1 Poetic Reappraisals

1　Cultural Hybridity in David Dabydeen's Poetry　3
MONICA MANOLACHI

2　Living Beadless in a Foreign Land: David Dabydeen's Poetry of Disappearance　15
ANJALI NERLEKAR

3　Fresh Names: Audience, Authenticity and the African Imaginary in *Turner* and *A Harlot's Progress*　30
NICOLE MATOS

Part 2 (Re)reading the Novels

4　Translating *The Intended*　43
JENNY DE SALVO

5　Intertextuality and the "Spatialization" of Reading: Conradian Journeys in Dabydeen's *Disappearance*　58
RUSSELL WEST-PAVLOV

Contents

6   David Dabydeen's *A Harlot's Progress*: Re-presenting the Slave Narrative Genre   73
    ABIGAIL WARD

7   "To Say Profitably": Dabydeen's Exoticist Aesthetic   84
    ERIK FALK

8   Re-scripting Genealogies, or, On the Purpose of (Re)writing in David Dabydeen's *Our Lady of Demerara*   101
    LILIANA SIKORSKA

9   "Everything Is Illuminated": Trauma, Literary Alchemy and Transfiguration in David Dabydeen's *Molly and the Muslim Stick*   116
    JUTTA SCHAMP

10 The Magic of Your Making: Magic and Realism in David Dabydeen's Recent Fiction   136
    MICHAEL MITCHELL

    Contributors   151

Introduction

LYNNE MACEDO

Talking Words: New Essays on the Work of David Dabydeen contains the most recent collection of critical writing that is focused exclusively on the fictional output of this acclaimed poet and novelist. Its publication has been designed to coincide with that of *Pak's Britannica: Interviews and Articles by David Dabydeen,* and to offer a fresh but complementary look at all of Dabydeen's major works by Caribbean scholars from across the world. Each of the chapters in *Talking Words* was specially commissioned or, with one exception, extensively revised for inclusion in this book. Collectively, they are able to give new insights into both Dabydeen's earlier poetry and the six novels he has published to date. The range, scope and originality of these chapters clearly demonstrate the continuing interest in critical appraisal of all of Dabydeen's writing.

Born on a sugar plantation in Berbice, Guyana, Dabydeen moved to England as a teenager and attended school in south London. He won a scholarship to read English at Cambridge and graduated with an honours degree in 1978, followed by a PhD from University College, London, in 1982. During his time as a student, Dabydeen began writing poetry and experimenting with the use of Creole, influenced by his reading of medieval alliterative poetry.[1] His reputation as a creative writer was quickly established with the publication of this work in *Slave Song* (1984), and led to his first literary awards: the Quiller-Couch Prize and the Commonwealth Poetry Prize.

Slave Song received critical attention not just for its language and exploration of the lives of Indo-Guyanese "coolies", but also for the provocative manner in which Dabydeen parodied Eliot's *The Waste Land* through the use of Standard English "translations" of his poems. *Coolie Odyssey* followed in

Introduction

1988 and, in contrast to his first volume of poetry, was largely composed in Standard English. The poems in this collection explored notions of identity and what it meant to be exiled from a Caribbean homeland, and were shortlisted for the Geoffrey Faber Memorial Prize. *Turner* was then published in 1994, and featured a long title poem of the same name which gave voice to the submerged head of the African slave in the foreground of the renowned *Slave Ship* painting by J.M.W. Turner. Although *Turner* provoked controversy and quickly became the subject of numerous critical readings,[2] it remains Dabydeen's last major poetic publication to date.

Since the early 1990s, Dabydeen's fictional writing has found outlet through the novel format, although his choice of material and skilful use of language have clear parallels with his earlier poetry. His first novel, *The Intended*, was published in 1991, and in 1992 it won Dabydeen the first of three Guyana Prizes for Literature. It concerns a young, nameless narrator who compares his happy childhood in Guyana with his stark existence as a student in England, and clearly carries parallels to Dabydeen's own life. The importance of this journey from the Caribbean to England is re-enacted in his second novel, *Disappearance* (1993), which has another, nameless narrator who arrives in Hastings from Guyana to help shore up the crumbling coastline. The engineer's continual struggles to find some real sense of identity have, as Dabydeen freely acknowledges, conscious echoes of themes that were explored in V.S. Naipaul's *The Enigma of Arrival* (1987). It is apparent that both of these early novels carry allusions to Conrad's *Heart of Darkness* (1899), a work to which Dabydeen has often referred as a source of influence on his writing.

There is a marked stylistic change in his next two novels – *The Counting House* (1996) and *A Harlot's Progress* (1999) – as they both have a historical context. The former novel explores the system of indentureship through two main characters whose lives are corrupted when they migrate from India to work on a sugar plantation in nineteenth century British Guiana. *A Harlot's Progress* won Dabydeen a second Guyana Prize for Literature in 2000 and has similarities to his poem *Turner*, insofar as he takes inspiration from a series of paintings by Hogarth to provide a framework for this eighteenth-century narrative.[3] By deliberately drawing attention to the ambiguous narration of "Mungo", the black servant boy in Hogarth's painting, Dabydeen highlights the fictional constructs of not just the "slave narrative" genre but this very novel itself. Mungo's inability to present the "truth" about his past demonstrates how the history of slavery must remain an enigma that can never be fully understood, or confined to the pages of a book.

There is a further dramatic shift in Dabydeen's two latest novels, both of which contain an ecological "message" about the redemptive nature of the Guyanese interior.[4] *Our Lady of Demerara* (2004) clearly pays homage to Dabydeen's fellow Guyanese writer Wilson Harris, and was awarded the Guyana Prize for Literature in that same year. It explores the reverse journey *from* Britain to the Caribbean through a narrative that deals with an unlikely couple named Lance and Elizabeth, whose lives become entangled with the tale of two Irish priests: Father Wilson and Father Harris. In *Molly and the Muslim Stick* Dabydeen tackles sexual abuse and religious fundamentalism through another unlikely group of characters: Molly, the victimized white woman from Lancashire; Apotu-Om, a Guyanese Amerindian; and the shape-shifting Muslim walking-stick of the novel's title. In their quest for self-fulfilment, Molly and Stick travel to the Guyanese interior – as does Lance in *Our Lady of Demerara* – on a journey full of transformative possibilities.

In order to deal with such a diverse body of writing, *Talking Words* has been divided into two sections, each of which contains chapters whose focus is predominantly on one aspect of Dabydeen's writing – his poetry or his novels. In part 1 there are three chapters that engage primarily with Dabydeen's poems, which examine how the application of theory can hide as much as it reveals;[5] re-evaluate his ambivalence towards national identity and historical representation; and explore the African imaginary in both *Turner* and the novel *A Harlot's Progress*. All of the contributors in this section have tackled his poetry from different perspectives, but their chapters are thematically linked by the ways in which they identify the many contradictions inherent in Dabydeen's writing.

The main focus of the first chapter is on hybridity and cultural identity – two issues that have a particular resonance when dealing with any aspect of Dabydeen's writing, but which Monica Manolachi argues are particularly relevant to his poetry. By exploring the connections between hybridity and hubris and the ways in which Dabydeen employs the latter "as a source of energy" (p. 12), Manolachi suggests that the cultural hybridity displayed in his poems is far more complex than a simple "cross-cultural exchange" between binary opposites. Using examples from all three volumes of poetry, she demonstrates how different kinds of hybridity are manifest in his work –

whether it is linguistic hybridity, thematic hybridity, or the assimilation and blending of multiple cultures, characters and religions that takes place in *Turner*. The skilfulness of Dabydeen's poetry, she asserts, lies in its transformative and varied nature which "challenges previous characterizations of the Caribbean" (p. 5).

In the second chapter, Anjali Nerlekar examines the complex relationship between Dabydeen's writing and the notion of "Indianness", arguing that the ambiguous nature of his poetry suggests "an inability to neither completely embrace nor totally reject the indentured past of his community and the colonized history of Guyana" (p. 15).[6] Furthermore, despite his appropriation from aspects of a Caribbean, English and Indian past in an effort to find some new kind of identity, Nerlekar asserts that ultimately Dabydeen's poetry "shows this attempt at elision to be a failure" (p. 16). Through illustrations from *Turner* which highlight Dabydeen's concept of a "common ancestry", or his utilization of Guyanese Creole in *Slave Song*, she argues that the "repeated blending" of ethnicities is largely an imaginative project that belies the reality of "the ethnic violence of his native Guyana" (p. 25). Eventually, this erasure of traditional boundaries and identities appears to have led to the ultimate "disappearance" of "*any* identifiable self", which, as the closing words of *Turner* suggest, is "both a freeing experience and an experience of utter deprivation and loneliness" (p. 27).

The third and final chapter in this section provides a series of connections between Dabydeen's poetry and his fiction, as the author shows how aspects of his narrative poem *Turner* have a direct link to the novel *A Harlot's Progress*. Nicole Matos is concerned with the ways in which writing about slavery can be potentially "stultified through excess, crushed and overburdened with preconceived signs" (p. 30), and how Dabydeen consciously tries to avoid these pitfalls. She begins by identifying three separate "levels of invention" (p. 31) that Dabydeen employs when describing the many "African" memories located in *Turner*, and then demonstrates how this mixture of real, imaginary and "misplaced" names has been deliberately constructed to destabilize the reader's quest for exoticism. After acknowledging the influence of Equiano on *Turner*, and how the veracity of *his* narrative has been the subject of recent debate, Matos then turns her attention towards *A Harlot's Progress* to suggest that Dabydeen has used similar concerns about authenticity to again confound the reader. Instead of presenting an "authentic" account of his life, Mungo's narrative turns into "a parodic stream of regurgitated textualisms" (p. 35). She concludes by showing how Dabydeen's strategy serves to remind the reader of their secret desire for the exoticized other, but that this is something which is "simply beyond the power of our shared narrative to provide" (p. 37).

In the second section of *Talking Words*, the main focus shifts towards an appraisal of Dabydeen's novels and includes, for the first time, a chapter concerned with the complexities of translating his earliest novel, *The Intended*. Three other chapters in this section each deal with one or more of the earlier works, examining intertextual readings of *Disappearance*, reading *A Harlot's Progress* as a re-working of the slave narrative genre, and exploring how the theme of narrative commodification can be traced throughout *all* of Dabydeen's novels. The final three chapters of *Talking Words* are concerned with Dabydeen's two most recent novels, both of which are partly set in Guyana. By using a narrative style in which identities shift and transform, Dabydeen hints that redemption may be found in that very particular landscape, even for characters whose lives have been indelibly marked by various forms of abuse and crime. Each of the three chapters tackles these complex novels from a different perspective, although collectively they show how both works engage in a dialogue with memory, history and estrangement. They bring the reader up to date with Dabydeen's development as a novelist, while also highlighting new developments in critical thinking about Caribbean and black British writing.

Part 2 of *Talking Words* begins with a chapter that has been written from the perspective of a translator, and consequently its primary areas of concern are somewhat different to the other critical readings contained in this collection. Although Jenny de Salvo discusses intertextuality, which is also the main focus of chapter 5, her interest is necessarily from a linguistic perspective, as is her detailed exploration of "the variety of registers and languages" (p. 44) that Dabydeen employs in *The Intended*. By highlighting his numerous allusions to canonical works such as Blake's poem *The Tiger*, Wordsworth's preface to *Lyrical Ballads*, or Conrad's *Heart of Darkness*, she clearly demonstrates the subversive qualities of Dabydeen's novel, and the need for translation to work within the specific context of irony. De Salvo then provides a close examination of selected passages from *The Intended* together with examples of translation strategies that deal with its specific grammar and syntax, to pinpoint the methods by which Dabydeen blends and manipulates a mixture of languages to differentiate his main characters. She closes by considering how the novel's title might be translated in a way that retains its link back to Conrad's novella, while also attracting the Italian reader to Dabydeen's first novel.

Chapter 5 deals with Dabydeen's second novel *Disappearance*, and its examination of intertextual connections – in particular those with Conrad's *Heart of Darkness* – leads on from de Salvo's analysis of *The Intended*. Russell West-Pavlov argues that while Dabydeen entices "the informed reader to look for intertextual allusions" (p. 59) to Conrad in this novel, at the same time he deliberately frustrates that search. Although there appear to be parallels between characters such as Kurtz and Curtis, in *Disappearance* Dabydeen seems less interested in "a real engagement with *Heart of Darkness* in the manner of the earlier novel *The Intended*" (p. 60). By comparing the ways in which the journey motif is used in both works, West-Pavlov asserts that its form is incomplete in Dabydeen's novel; it is wrenched and lacking in "structural neatness" and fails to return to its starting point. Ironically, instead of yielding meaning, both the narrator's and ultimately the reader's "journey" to trace intertextual connections in *Disappearance* is "a round trip which results in a dispersal of meaning rather than its gathering up in a moment of re-assembly" (p. 68). His conclusion, however, is that the novel's lack of closure should *not* be read as an absence of substance, but rather as an illustration of how Dabydeen skilfully uses the concept of the "incomplete" journey to provide him with the "possibility of cultural renewal and artistic creativity" (p. 71).

Abigail Ward's chapter has connections to that of Matos's considered earlier, insofar as she provides a reading of *A Harlot's Progress* as a "re-presentation" of the slave narrative genre. However, her main area of concern is, in contrast, to interrogate the ways in which that genre of writing exploited the very people it was ostensibly designed to help, and how Dabydeen's novel suggests that "the twentieth-century casting of slave narrators as icons may be seen as another form of enslavement" (p. 81). By showing how slave narratives can be paralleled with a more recent trend in remembering "the early black British presence" (p. 74), she contends that Dabydeen's writing demonstrates the need for this subject to be handled sensitively if it is to avoid the pitfall of encouraging "morbid fascination or voyeuristic titillation at reading stories of bondage and cruelty exercised against black people" (p. 74). By linking the voyeuristic aspects of reading with a desire for images such as those provided by the artists Turner and Hogarth, Ward argues that Dabydeen is underlining the inherent need for the "sensational or pornographic" that has always informed the representation of black people in Britain. But, by stressing Mungo's resistance to the appropriation of his particular story, *A Harlot's Progress* reminds us that slaves were complex individuals, not a homogenous group, and that only by recognizing this can we begin "lightening the burden of representation" (p. 81) imposed upon black people, even today.

Chapter 7 of *Talking Words* provides an overview not just of Dabydeen's earlier fiction, but also touches upon his poetry and his most recent novel, *Molly and the Muslim Stick*. Erik Falk suggests that it is possible to trace a common theme of "connected economies of value, money and sentiment" (p. 85) in all of Dabydeen's fictional output, but one which serves to both display *and* undercut the notion of an "exoticist aesthetic". Through an interrogation of recent scholarship on the "postcolonial exotic", he shows that Dabydeen's writing is often "engaged in a double act" that hides as much as it displays, sometimes exploiting cultural difference (as in *Coolie Odyssey*) and other times resisting it, as in *The Intended*. Furthermore, in both *Turner* and *A Harlot's Progress*, Falk argues, the complexities of the writing are such that they both foreground cultural difference and yet refuse to abide by the constraints of such representation. Paradoxically, he suggests that in *Molly and the Muslim Stick* Dabydeen has employed exoticism not to capitalize upon his own cultural position, but rather as a literary device for transforming the "*relatively familiar* . . . into something foreign and strange" (p. 95). He concludes that while criticism on the "postcolonial exotic" is a welcome development, Dabydeen's writing has moved beyond a straightforward negotiation of exotic imagery, because it actually operates at a time when there no longer exists any "idea of authentic cultural difference, even as memory" (p. 98).

Chapter 8 focuses on *Our Lady of Demerara*, and examines the ways in which Dabydeen's penultimate novel deals with issues of identity. Through a detailed exploration of the characters of Lance and Elizabeth (Beth), who continually search for some sense of "belonging", Liliana Sikorska asserts that they cannot be viewed as "finite products; rather, they are emblematic of the course of reconstruction of identities" (p. 102). Dabydeen's novel is not, however, primarily concerned with hybridity, which is itself an unstable and changing concept. Instead, Sikorska contends that the instability of Elizabeth and Lance's identities is intertwined with Dabydeen's vision of history that is "always mutable" (p. 112). She concludes that the deliberately fractured nature of *Our Lady of Demerara*, with its "incongruous monologues, memory lapses and necessary omissions" (p. 112), serves to show that there is no "truth" about the past that can somehow be retrieved, no matter how hard one looks for it.

There are clear parallels to be drawn between the theme of a quest for self-realization and the fragmentary nature of both *Our Lady of Demerara* and *Molly and the Muslim Stick*. However, although Jutta Schamp's chapter identifies connections between the two works, she is mainly interested in the intertextual nature of Dabydeen's latest novel, and how the author "transfigures trauma and human suffering" (p. 117) through allusions to other writers. By illustrating the close thematic links with his fellow Guyanese Wilson Harris, Schamp suggests that Dabydeen's writing follows the former's "anti-realist tradition" by showing how "human beings have the gift of coping . . . through self-expression and transformation in dreams" (p. 118). The gradual transformation which takes place in the character of Molly has, she argues, strong links to a spiritual or religious concept, albeit one that is an eclectic mixture of Christian and Hindu symbols that have largely been "cleansed" of their colonial auras. In common with Lance in *Our Lady of Demerara*, what Molly finds in Guyana is anything but an Arcadian dream; instead she is "exposed to cyclical and cataclysmic Demerara mythology . . . [and] feels intimidated by the overwhelming presence and inexorability of the jungle" (p. 126). Even the ending of the novel, Schamp asserts, has been deliberately constructed by Dabydeen to subvert the reader's expectations. Instead of providing closure or self-fulfilment, Molly's journey continues on into the unknown, while it is Stick who is completely transfigured by becoming a literal part of the Guyanese jungle.

The concluding chapter in *Talking Words* looks at both of Dabydeen's latest novels, and suggests that any attempt at reading them as part of a realist tradition is doomed to failure. As an alternative, Michael Mitchell suggests that their combination of "brutally realistic elements" with others "described as absurdist or fantastic" might be considered a kind of magical realism. Through a detailed analysis of *Our Lady of Demerara*, Mitchell pinpoints both the complex forms of intertextuality that operate in that novel, and the numerous examples of "doubleness and ambivalence" in which "certainties . . . consume themselves in a play of opposites" (p. 139). He then examines some of the more obviously magical elements of *Molly and the Muslim Stick* and shows how that narrative operates largely "outside of the logic of realism". With its lack of causality, multiple perspectives and "playful seriousness", Dabydeen's most recent fiction does not, however, sit easily within existing definitions of magical realism. Mitchell's conclusion is that Dabydeen's very particular form of representation, one that is "dependent on the perceptions of reader and author as well as related events" (p. 147) is, therefore, more a form of "realist magicalism" that deliberately provokes the reader into seeking new ways of understanding.

At the time of writing this introduction, Dabydeen was working – as usual – on a new novel. If, as Mitchell contends, "something has definitely happened to David Dabydeen's [recent] novels" (p. 136), then it is hard to predict what form his next fiction will take, where it will be set, or how it will be received by the reading public. In an interview,[7] Dabydeen said that his next work will be a "green" novel, but that barely constitutes a clue as to what we might expect. There is really only one thing we can be certain of, if his previous six novels are anything to go by, which is that Dabydeen's fiction is unlikely to provide the reader with any easy answers.

Notes

1. Further details of Dabydeen's formative years as a writer can be found in several of the articles contained in the companion volume to this one, *Pak's Britannica: Articles by and Interviews with David Dabydeen*, ed. Lynne Macedo (Kingston: University of the West Indies Press, 2011).
2. See, for example, *No Land, No Mother* (Peepal Tree Press, 2007) which contains four essays on the title poem, or interviews with Kanaganayakam and Rainey in *Pak's Britannica*.
3. There are also direct links back to Dabydeen's own doctoral work on racial representations in eighteenth-century England.
4. See Dabydeen's interview with Gramaglia in *Pak's Britannica* for how he now views himself as a "green" writer.
5. See also Dabydeen's call for a move away from Eurocentric theory as a means of understanding Caribbean writing in "Teaching West Indian Literature in Britain", *Pak's Britannica*.
6. See also Dabydeen's views on "Indianness" and the need to avoid essentialism in several interviews in *Pak's Britannica*.
7. See interview with Gramaglia in *Pak's Britannica*.

Part 1

POETIC REAPPRAISALS

CHAPTER 1

Cultural Hybridity in David Dabydeen's Poetry

MONICA MANOLACHI

IN STUART HALL'S COGENT SYNTHESIS of the diasporic Caribbean cultural identity as essentially hybrid (1990) and set at the encounter between the (un)spoken, the (un)speakable and the (dis)covered, cultural hybridity[1] emerges as a heavy vacancy longing to be recognized, both as a place of negotiation and as one of collision. In this context, it is relevant that the DuBoisean idea of the "double consciousness" was reassessed by Paul Gilroy, who stated that dealing with different kinds of consciousness, originally African and American, implies a "special stress that grows with the effort involved in trying to face (at least) two ways at once" (1993, 3). Moreover, these concerns are in line with what Homi K. Bhabha defined as the "third space of enunciation, which makes the structure of meaning and reference an ambivalent process [. . . that] challenges our sense of the historical identity of culture as a homogenizing, unifying force", a "split space", "unrepresentable in itself" (1994, 38). Taking, as an example, the Guyanese writer Wilson Harris's "void" which is created at the confrontation of different cultures, Bhabha makes it clear that this "void" can be turned into an "in-between space [. . .] that carries the burden of the meaning of culture" (p. 38). This chapter aims to explore what is the source of this stress or burden, and what kind of energy is needed to carry it for artistic purposes. Such a phenomenon is neither singular nor specific to the Caribbean or to the twentieth century, but an awareness of its complexities is perhaps more evident in the postcolonial literature rooted in this region than in others. By examining the connection between hybridity and hubris[2] and by using illustrations from David Dabydeen's poems, it will be argued that exploring cultural hybridity is characterized by both rewards and limitations.

The *Oxford English Dictionary* states that the ultimate root of hybridity is, indeed, hubris, the ancient Greek ὕβρις. The connection between these terms has been reflected by the extensive use of hubris in the humanities – in history, literature and philosophy – where it refers to the transgression of social or divine boundaries that is followed by *nemesis* or retribution. To give an example of current usage, for the political analyst David Owen it is "an illness of *position* as much as of the *person*" (2007, 3; my emphasis). These terms are very much related to contemporary debates regarding cultural identity. M. Hård and A. Jamison (2005) explore the conflicting relationship between *hubris* and *hybrid* in their cultural history of technology and science, in the sense that only by taming the former and by becoming the latter can man advance, because hybridity has changed humanity's relation to nature. Experimentation has led to destruction and dislocation, and crisis has been internalized, which has important consequences for cultural matters as well.

What follows is an examination of the relationship between the transgressive force of hubris and the cultural theorists' concerns with the unbridled and objectionable features of hybridity. Although cultural hybridity has often been celebrated over the past decades, one question that may arise when these two concepts are placed together is what happens when different uncertainties and misinterpretations manifest themselves in different proportions in "the third space of enunciation". If the colonial experience was possible because of the fixed power relations between those in subject positions over those in object positions, then postcolonial conditions have produced a more versatile relationship in which the wearing of masks has been essential in understanding otherness. Identity play is significant for the representation of otherness particularly when the object is reduced to its abjection.[3] If we consider the Latin etymology of the abject, *ab-*, "away from" and *-ject*, "to throw", then throwing the self into an (un)desirable position, away from being and towards becoming something "unexpected" is an expression of the old concept of hubris. Characters in the ancient Greek dramas used to fall into hubris because they dared to arbitrarily transgress boundaries towards the divine or social laws, acts usually regarded as sins that were followed by retribution, either as reward or as punishment. In Dabydeen's poetry, such abjection is not simply nihilistic, but a carnivalesque source of laughter and catharsis, the fundamental aspect of an absorptive and yet creative process, and the ultimate frontier before metamorphosis.

In terms of spiritual geography, the three volumes of poetry published by Dabydeen so far, *Slave Song* (1984), *Coolie Odyssey* (1988) and *Turner* (1995), clearly map a long journey from India to Guyana, from Guyana to England, and then from England to Africa. This journey, both physical and spiritual, reflects a significant sense of family and ancestry and the need for belonging and for marking time in the context of various types of migration. As for the ranges of tonality employed, it is possible to trace a passage from a carnivalesque, humorous and emancipatory tone in the first volume to something more elegiac but still sometimes humorous in the second. In the third volume, however, there is a dramatic shift towards a more prophetic and dramatic tone. Dabydeen's poetry is born out of protest manifested at the confluence of different cultures, which challenges previous characterizations of the Caribbean, especially those relating to his own Indian origins. Rather than trying to circumscribe his poetic identity, this chapter traces its transformations by examining the role of hubris that such cultural hybridity entails, and explores the ways in which the poet resorts to it as a source of creative energy in order to release the tensions of fixed binary oppositions.

The poems in Creole in his first volume, *Slave Song*, accompanied by translations and what the poet calls "spoof notes"[4] (Binder 1989, 75), are supposed to articulate what standard English cannot express about the slaves' broken lives on plantations. E.A. Williams described the book as "a testament to the ravages of colonization" (1999, 106), but the poet distances himself from writing just a death-driven account, and aims at using what he calls "the erotic energies of the colonial experience, ranging from a corrosive to a lyrical sexuality" (p. 10), to emphasize what mental resistance could imply when physical resistance is impossible. By not being just an inhabitation of an "other" for the reader, his multi-layered perspective creates a space for authentic dialogue.

In "Song of the Creole Gang Women", the five different voices and their chorus are homogenized into only one when the poem is translated from Creole into English, producing an effect of simultaneous hybridity. This poem, as well as others, is a way of showing that "the subaltern can speak" (Spivak 1988) via an indirect, fragmented kind of communication. The intensity of the slave women's resistance is intensified by the metaphor of the "squashed crappau" (Dabydeen 2005, 39), a reference to the French influence in the Caribbean. The comparison of the women with the frogs as they are "about to leap" (p. 39) signifies the denial of becoming an ontological project as imposed by colonialism upon slaves. Several cultural aspects clash here, which reveal great insights regarding the ambivalence between accommodation and resistance that characterized life on the plantation. One is the old Hindu funeral custom of *sati*, when a widow used to sacrifice her life for her dead husband on his funeral pyre. Even though the poem is not about any particular husband, and this empty position is taken by Booker, the plantation owner, it still conveys his absence and degeneration. The women's ambiguous attitude towards the "pimpla", "a gigantic white thorn", which symbolizes both sexual abuse and colonial power, expresses their fascination and horror that is part of their fight against the system.

The production of such power cannot sustain a normal mother-child relationship, as their children "are strapped like burdens to [their] backs" and they wish to "shake off [their] babies" and "shake off [their] wombs" (p. 39) when they arrive at the river, where they seek release and spiritual freedom. The third woman's question, "Is true everything stall, gape, bleed, / Like crappau foot squash jess as e'ya leap?" (p. 18), is a reference to the theological and philosophical concept of the leap of faith, the act of believing in something without or in spite of empirical belief, a phrase attributed to the Danish philosopher Søren Kirkegaard. Nonetheless, here, it is prohibitively articulated, which suggests that the women slaves were trapped in the system and are doomed to be sacrificed. The tense uneasiness between the Christian and the Hindu religious paradigms is rendered by depicting a threatening environment: "sun in my eye like thorn", "the sun how it's fixed in the sky like a taskmaster's eye" (p. 39). Eventually, overwhelmed by the thought of being forced into sin and still fighting against their suicidal desire, the women's temporary relief is expressed by the ritual of the purificatory bathing in the river, an intertextual reference to the sacred Ganges river, mentioned in *Rig-Veda*.

Such toil is not present only at the level of the poetic personages. In Mark McWatt's review of *Slave Song*, one can identify the kinds of hubris both the author and his audience are prone to. Assuming the role of "messenger, translator, apologist, explicator" (1989, 87) does not involve simply wearing masks, but also creating them and, more importantly, bearing their burden. On the other hand, the English reader bears the burden of recognizing the need for cultural translation and an introduction into something that sounds like English, but is not.

By way of contrast, the use of Creole in Dabydeen's second collection, *Coolie Odyssey* (1988), is moderate, and the linguistic hybridity is taken over by the thematic hybridity with a more intensive and constant dialogue with the preceding corpus of English literary colonial productions in a perpetual challenge to earlier writing. This intratextual project, started in the first volume of poetry and characterized by fragmented and fractured discourses, intimates here the blurring of the interval between opposing symbols and a more visible attempt to heal the fracture.

In "Coolie Mother" (Dabydeen 1988, 16) and "Coolie Son" (p. 17), two separate poems talking to each other, the coolie mother's determination for her son not to "turn out like he rum-sucker chamar dadee" is indirectly voiced. Portraying the father figure in this way accentuates the dwarfed destiny assigned to the oppressed male by colonialism. The third person singular creates a space for dialogue, which is in contrast with the coolie son's first person epistolary discourse. Her failed leap of faith is rooted in the memory of the Ganges River, and her daily chore of fetching water is a form of identification with the river: "Fetch water, all day fetch water like if the whole- / Whole slow-flowing Canje river God create / Just for she one own bucket." She assumes the burden in the old way, as a sacrifice, and she is still marked by the stereotype of inferiority. Such an attitude is tragi-comically mirrored in the coolie son's letter, where to "turn lawya or dacta" is rendered as quite a far-fetched dream. Her faith that Harilall "*must* read book, / Learn talk proper" runs counter to the reality of his "reading book bad-bad" and his job as a "Deputy Sanitary Inspecta" (a toilet attendant), which criticizes the idea of England as the land of Cockaigne, with plenty of jobs for everyone. Her relentless hope in contrast with the coolie son's alarming smugness reiterates the "squashed crappau" and what can be called serious humour by the association with the slang "crap". In this way, the traces of abjection existing in their dialogue can be wiped out by the soothing memory of the sacred river, ironically associated here with the subtext of the flushing water of modern toilets. The humorous effect created by releasing the energy of the anxiety involved negates the sadness of such a reality.

In this context, the *sati* woman, who was heard in the first volume of poetry, appears here with a more articulated voice in contrast with the white woman's voice and image in the poems inspired by *The Tempest*. Nevertheless, the contrast is not absolute, because the hybridity of the "rare conceits" (p. 13) intervenes, so that these voices become more indistinct. There is also a whole phenomenology of absorption between the postcolonial male subject and the woman as literary otherness, intended to grasp and represent who assimilates what object, with a rhetoric of inclusion, belonging and possession versus one of separation, abandon and dispossession. In "Water With Berries",[5] for instance, we learn "he fleshed her frame of waste / Sucked her distress" during "A long night of instant love / In which he spent her sense of pain / Lapped at her ego / Like the mouth of beasts / Met in darkness at water's edge" (p. 36). This last image is an obvious echo of the ancient Greek concern with hybridity, a significant detail which illustrates the poet's commitment to display as many facets of the phenomenon as possible. To be more precise, H.M. Feinberg and J.B. Solodow show that the origin of the saying "there is always something new out of Africa" goes back to antiquity, and they note: "Aristotle attributes the large variety of hybrids in Africa to the different species meeting at watering holes and mating indiscriminately [. . .] because of the lack of water" (2002, 257). Even though, in ancient Greece, the phrase had a biologically negative interpretation, the authors draw attention to its current positive one. Dabydeen's transference of this old tale to a modern love affair is meant both to unshackle stereotypical views regarding postcolonial anxieties, and to employ the energies they entail.

This discourse of absorption is paralleled by a discourse of silence hiding shame. The "muted claws of empire" (Dabydeen 1988, 10) representing the corner shop's English customers who still nurture an exotic perspective on the Caribbean are contrasted with the East Indians' silence expressed by Chandra's shame of getting pregnant, while Old Dabydeen just "stamped and cursed" and kept himself busy by "dreaming of India". Dabydeen's poetic project has been to break these mutual silences among Caribbean family members that have made their shame unbearable. The agents of breaking the silence are the migrant coolies themselves, with "their faces and best saris black with soot . . . / plotting / in the packed bowel of a white man's boat", like difficult babies in their mother's womb. Chandra's shame at getting pregnant is in stark contrast too with Miranda's mothering promise to "blot out the tyrant sun" (p. 33). At least optically, the latter's silhouette against the sun would most probably look darker. By way of blurring the difference, she is thus "a new mother" not in an essentialist way, because her delusive promise is a hybrid attraction, "a fantasy" akin to the ancient Greek belief regarding the sense of "something new" – strangeness, revolution, undesirability or even evil – and close to Ania Loomba's idea of "little Mirandas" (2002, 33) as the fruit of interbreeding. This is sustained also by the fact that, in front of the white woman, the sexually and linguistically impotent male subject "bled in deference" (Dabydeen 1988, 31) or, perhaps better, "in difference", which is more thought-provoking and culturally productive because it subtly reassesses the essentialist side of cultural hybridity by claiming that something has been lost.

This antagonistic relationship is more nuanced in "Caliban" (p. 34), written in the form of the aubade medieval tradition. Here, the woman's whiteness may not necessarily refer to skin or to a certain kind of spiritual knowledge: "womb of myth, foundry or funeral pyre / Where like a Hindu corpse I burn and shrink / To be reborn to your desire" is a description which bears the burden of hybridity lightly, "straining" and "craving", yet with the desire for further spiritual transgressions. In comparison with other previous postcolonial rewritings of Shakespeare's play, Dabydeen's poems do not simply "invert and appropriate the perspectives of *The Tempest*, most prominently by identifying with the bitter cursing of Caliban", as Elleke Boehmer (2005, 196) contends, because this would be just another perpetuation of irreconcilable opposites. Perhaps it should be better acknowledged that the dialogism of Dabydeen's poetry has contributed to the formulation of the tertiary space, which allows concomitant essentialist and universalist literary strategies and readings.

Along with some of the other poems in the first volumes, *Turner* (1995) renders an unknown side of the cultural identity of the Black Atlantic, in which the image of the slave drowning from J.M.W. Turner's painting *Slave Ship* is represented by Dabydeen in a different light. Yet the scope of the poem goes beyond the geographical limits of Gilroy's syntagma, because, apart from the European-American-African cultural environment, the multi-level and intertextual discourse reveals the clash and interpenetration of Western, Asian and African systems of thought and beliefs, with the effect of blurring boundaries. It also goes beyond the aesthetic aspects which the association between the poem and the painting may imply, and which have been the subject of previous interpretations. As Abigail Ward points out, "instead of promoting a visual representation of slavery, [the poet] indicates in 'Turner' through the metaphor of blindness that a verbal (written) approach might be a more helpful way of thinking about this past" (2007, 50), which is in line with pursuing the "dream that the world know word" (Dabydeen 1988, 41).

Even though most of the plots of its narrative seem to be set somewhere near and in Africa, the multiple split subject of the poem assimilates various references to other cultural locations (European, Caribbean, Indian) to blend some of their values and to forge an identity which at the beginning is "stillborn from all the signs": "What was deemed mere food for sharks will become / My fable" (p. 9). The double signification involved here is close to Kristeva's notion of the abject, neither subject nor object, something that exists and yet does not. To the abject, the forgotten unshackled African slave, who receives the name Turner, Dabydeen opposes the "longed-for gift of motherhood" (p. 9), a tension that shows the bearing of the burden in different ways, either as being a failure, a loss, a corruptive undertaking, a fortunate labour or an artistic work. The "woman giving birth, belly / Blown and flapping loose and torn like sails" and "The part-born, sometimes with its mother / Tossed overboard" (p. 9) reveal harrowing stories of wasted energies, out of which the fable develops. Because the hubris of the slave owners during the Middle Passage era is heavy, it is shared by other characters in a composite, hybrid role. Thus, Turner is also the name of the captain of the ship, the initiator of degeneration; it is the name of the baby tossed overboard, the bearer of innocence, unable to remember; and it is the moniker the author appropriates to play upon the words and turn the tables on the artist J.M.W. Turner. The *I* of the African, as the poet mentions in his notes, "invents a body, a biography and peoples an imagined landscape" (p. 10), makes up names for the fauna and flora around itself and creates gods to worship, such as "Sensu courting Zein" (p. 13), a possible wordplay for *meaning* courting *being*, if we admit Sensu is another name for "sense" and Zein another name for the German "Sein".

Apart from what is skilfully invented, however, one can trace aspects of Hindu and Caribbean cultures such as the symbolism of the sacred cow and the "backdam of my mother's house". Yet, the sacredness of the cow is ambiguous, both caring and threatening. The children's play under the belly of the cow, which has "covetous eyes", suggests danger and corruption, while the milking of the cow is an expression of the colonial power milking the colonies and of the colonized submissively accepting it. Nonetheless, there is a recurrence in preserving the symbol, when the image of Krishna depicted as a child who protects the cows is echoed by "I sit in the savannah minding cows" and when the mother is evoked in "My mother / Watches over me, eyes big like our cow's / But full of sadness" (p. 12).

After the ordeal of separating the family members and of boarding them on ships, the complex subject of the poem is loaded with the identity of the stillborn tossed overboard, an "agent of self-recognition", as mentioned in the preface. Because the relationship between the colonizer and the colonized is destined to failure, the white man's burden of civilizing the rest of the world is severely criticized in the metaphor of the children who are mirrored in the sailor's boots: "the black leather boots which he lets us / Polish, till we can see our faces. / Each day boys scramble at his feet, fighting / To clean them first" (p. 14). This mirroring involves the danger of being kicked in the face, and is in stark contrast with the psychoanalytical concept of the "mirror role" of the mother developed by D. Winnicott (1971, 144).

The mother figure does not appear anymore as in the previous volumes; there are no mongrel Mirandas, no coolie mothers, no *Mas* this time, all previously associated with traditional cultural roots. This makes the creative process take another, more mythical route. The voice of the abject is projected into the realm of the imagination that is conveyed by "the belly of moon". The abject is thus transferred to a non-defined exterior, from where it calls the now awakened subject twice, which evinces restructuring of their relationship: "'Nigger,' it cries, naming me from some hoard / Of superior knowledge", "'Nigger,' / It cries, sensing its own deformity", "I stare / Into its face as into a daedal / Seed" (Dabydeen 2002, 31). These last words are a reference to the myth of Daedalus, the builder of the labyrinth, where the monstrous Minotaur was secretly kept, another example of the connection existing between hybrid and hubris in Greek mythology, a reminder that creation requires sacrifice, and a dialogue between Greek mythology and the sacredness of the Hindu cow.

Although the poem ends with the negation of creation and of origins,[6] "No stars, no land, no words, no community, / No mother" (p. 42) as a reverse or a reading back of the holy books, the theme here is of cultural hybridity accompanied by all the anxieties it may entail. The wish for a new beginning composed of disparate (un)consciousnesses reminds us of the original sacrifice in many world religions. As a postcolonial poet, Dabydeen summons in *Turner* the dispersed pre-colonial past and invests emotional energy in it, but not without exploring first its diversity and the intricacies of this site of memory which he wishes to transform into an inhabitable home.

What I have argued in this chapter is that the fragile wish "to begin anew in the sea" (p. 41) is based on linguistic and aesthetic play and a rich chronotopic intertextuality,[7] and necessitates hubris as a source of energy. The burden of transgressing boundaries, of sexuality and racial difference as other facets of colonial desire, are all linked by the poet to aspects of his Caribbean experience: "It takes generations before people really understand and accept each other, certainly at the sexual level, the family level" (Binder 1989, 68). The passage from the carnivalesque to the elegiac and to the prophetic discourse which is apparent throughout these three volumes suggests an attempt to break the old opposition between Prospero and Caliban, and to allow the metamorphosis of an abject into a subject by the objectification inherent in the creative process. However, such a hybrid identity is necessarily accompanied by anxieties, and does not offer an easy or comfortable form of "newness".

Therefore, cultural hybridity is not simply some form of cross-cultural exchange, because this perspective can mask cultural disparities and incongruence, giving a wrong impression of their symmetry. Neither abusing the term, which involves the perpetuation of the binaries hybridity should replace, nor moving beyond it, which implies reducing cultural divisions to none, seem, in Dabydeen's view, to be completely successful paths to take. Even though either of the two can be temporarily strategically employed, they are sometimes seen as opposites of another theoretical trap. By exploring how cultures influence each other and examining the features and conditions of the hybridization phenomena, Dabydeen's poetry suggests that the anxiety of encountering the possibly conflictual unknown can be made more bearable.

Notes

1. As a postcolonial concept, cultural hybridity has been the subject of debate over several decades, and cultural theorists have been trying to grasp its force by explaining some of its features in the domain of cultural politics and its effects upon cultural identity. However, if one considers contemporary cultural productions in liminal spaces more closely, there are still numerous questions that inevitably arise when hybridity is at stake.

2. Hubris is one of the most familiar ancient Greek words. When approaching ancient Greek literary, philosophical and legal texts, D.M. MacDowell concludes: "(a) Hubris has various causes and various manifestations, but fundamentally it is having energy or power and misusing it self-indulgently. (b) It is the same thing in literature and in law, except that the law is not interested in an act of hubris unless another human being is the victim of it" (1976, 30). A more recent work on this subject is N.R.E. Fisher's *A Study in the Values of Honour and Shame in Ancient Greece* (1992).
3. Julia Kristeva defined abjection as a state of being "neither subject nor object", a name without "a definable object", a "weight of meaninglessness, about which there is nothing insignificant, and which crushes me [. . .] a reality that, if I acknowledge it, annihilates me" (1982, 2).
4. These notes are explanatory to a certain extent, but they also ironically comment on the tradition of glossary notes that work rather to obscure than to clarify, as in T.S. Eliot's *The Waste Land*; all this with the purpose of expanding what was once obfuscated by, for example, John Ruskin's footnote regarding J.M.W. Turner's *Slave Ship*.
5. Intertextuality with the title of George Lamming's novel *Water with Berries* (1971).
6. This ending may be interpreted as a reiteration and reinterpretation of the difficulty of admitting the traumatic separation of the black people from Africa via cultural hybridity. Other Caribbean poets such as James Berry approached the subject: "I have never seen you, Africa . . . / Any wonder I have no love for you?" he writes in his poem "In Our Year 1941 My Letter to Mother Africa" (1995, 34).
7. By employing the Bakhtinian notion of "chronotope", what is meant here refers to the restructuring and transforming impact of intertextuality on the spatio-temporal matrix the poems refer to, intertextuality understood as "the transposition of one or more systems of signs into another, accompanied by a new articulation of the enunciative and denotative position" (Kristeva 1980, 15).

References

Berry, J. 1995. *Hot Earth Cold Earth*. Newcastle upon Tyne: Bloodaxe Books (orig. pub. 1985).
Bhabha, H.K. 1994. *The Location of Culture*. London: Routledge.
Binder, W. 1989. "Interview with David Dabydeen". *Journal of West Indian Literature* 3, no. 2: 67–80.
Boehmer, E. 2005. *Colonial and Postcolonial Literature: Migrant Metaphors*. Oxford: Oxford University Press.
Dabydeen, D. 1988. *Coolie Odyssey*. Hertford: Hansib.

———. 2002. *Turner : New and Selected Poems*. Leeds: Peepal Tree Press.
———. 2005. *Slave Song*. Leeds: Peepal Tree Press.
Feinberg, H.M., and J.B. Solodow. 2002. "Out of Africa". *Journal of African History* 43, no. 2: 255–61.
Gilroy, P. 1993. *The Black Atlantic: Modernity and Double Consciousness*. London: Verso.
Hall, S. 1990. "Cultural Identity and Diaspora". In *The Post-Colonial Studies Reader,* ed. B. Ashcroft, G. Griffiths, and H. Tiffin, 435–38. London: Routledge.
Hård, M., and A. Jamison. 2005. *Hubris and Hybrids: A Cultural History of Technology and Science.* New York: Routledge.
Kristeva, J. 1980. *Desire in Language: A Semiotic Approach to Literature and Art*. Oxford: Blackwell.
———. 1982. *The Powers of Horror: An Essay on Abjection.* New York: Columbia University Press.
Loomba, A. 2002. *Shakespeare, Race and Colonialism.* Oxford: Oxford University Press.
MacDowell, D.M. 1976. "'Hubris' in Athens". *Greece and Rome,* Second Series 23, no. 1: 14–31.
McWatt, M. 1989. Review. *Journal of West Indian Literature* 3, no. 2: 86–90.
Owen, D. 2007. *The Hubris Syndrome: Bush, Blair and the Intoxication of Power*. London: Politico's.
Spivak, G.C. 1988. "Can the Subaltern Speak?" In *Marxism and the Interpretation of Culture,* ed. C. Nelson and L. Grossberg, 271–313. London: Macmillan.
Ward, A. 2007. "'Words Are All I Have Left of My Eyes': Blinded by the Past in J.M.W. Turner's *Slavers Throwing Overboard the Dead and Dying* and David Dabydeen's 'Turner'". *Journal of Commonwealth Literature* 42, no. 1: 47–58.
Williams, E.A. 1999. *Poetic Negotiations of Identity in the Works of Brathwaite, Harris, Senior and Dabydeen: Tropical Paradise Lost and Regained.* Lewiston, NY: Edwin Mellen Press.
Winnicott, D.W. 1971. *Playing and Reality.* Harmondsworth: Penguin.

CHAPTER 2

Living Beadless in a Foreign Land
David Dabydeen's Poetry of Disappearance

ANJALI NERLEKAR

DAVID DABYDEEN IS ONE OF THE most visible writers from the Caribbean to foreground the Indian heritage of the Indo-Caribbeans, and yet his work professes an intriguing and conflicted relation with the idea of "Indianness". Even while his poetry attempts to valorize the Indo-Guyanese self, it also betrays an ambivalence towards its colonial past with the British and its indentured roots in India. The endeavour to resurrect the Indo- in the Guyanese is not an attempt to reach a mythic pre-colonial Indian past; rather, the Indian connection enables Dabydeen to solidify his Guyanese identity. In both national and regional affiliations, Dabydeen adopts an extremely slippery exterior.

Dabydeen's poetry achieves this state of flux by its problematic refusal *and* acceptance of one's history. Through a mixing of the lineages and chronologies of the various ethnicities that comprise Guyana, and by destroying the boundary between Guyana and England, this poetry implies an innate ambivalence towards national identity and national pasts. His work points to an inability to neither completely embrace nor totally reject the indentured past of his community and the colonized history of Guyana. Hence his continuous motion between the various pasts; the oppositions between Creole and English that negate each other; and the gory highlighting of violence and rape in his work, even as he stops the reader from walking away with a singular understanding of this act.

Dabydeen's poetry presents a very complex approach to the past of his community and his national history. Both in the postscript to *Slave Song* and in the poems in *Coolie Odyssey*, the poet expressly states his discomfort with his own project of writing his past. *Coolie Odyssey* opens with a poem that takes a contemptuous look at his own work that seems to fall into the ever-popular enterprise of using folk or peasant history as a means to fame and riches. Consequently, in self-destructive irony, the narrator says, let me take advantage of this and sell the poverty of my tribe to the reader:

> Now that peasantry is in vogue,
> Poetry bubbles from peat bogs,
> People strain for the old folks' fatal gobs
> Coughed up in grates North or North East
> 'Tween bouts o' living dialect,
> It should be time to hymn your own wreck,
> Your house the source of ancient song
> (Dabydeen 1988, 9)

It is this holographic comprehension of his depiction of the colonized past that is the groundbreaking aspect of Dabydeen's work. It is excitement always tinged with grief, a statement that perennially folds in on itself. Perhaps Dabydeen says it best when he talks about his merging of histories in his work: "it frees you up to then say, 'I have no past.' Now, that's not a glorious freedom, because it's still immersed in a kind of sorrow over what has been lost" (Dawes 2001, 197).

The two kinds of insubstantial selves, one in Guyana and the other in England, stand at the extremes of a continuum that begins historically in India and ends on English shores, and the poet highlights a set of desperate measures to break this progression from one kind of shadowy existence to another. The poet appropriates the gender role of women for the colonized male; the slave status from the Afro-Caribbean; English language and the English literary and artistic tradition from England; ideas of family and food habits from his Indian heritage; and the plantation experience from Guyana. And this attempt to give birth to a new identity of the Indo-Guyanese writer involves a violent yoking of conventional categories. But this binding of selves is only a temporary measure because, in the end, each poetic work shows this attempt at elision to be a failure.

India in the Caribbean

The official abolition of slavery in the colonies by the British administration in the mid-nineteenth century marked the beginning of another crossing of the waters, when indentured labourers from India were chosen to replace the newly emancipated slaves on the sugar plantations in the Caribbean, starting with Guyana in 1838. These were mostly poor, illiterate and marginalized people from India who were seen as convenient scapegoats for the imperial design to acquire cheap and secure labour.[1] They ended up living in practically segregated and insular communities because of the policies of the British administration that restricted them to the plantations. They were also thrown together in this bounded communal setting because of the hatred they faced from the Afro-Guyanese, who saw in them the replacements of their pre-abolition jobs, and hence a tool of perpetuation of the British hegemony over the country. For the Indo-Guyanese workers, it was almost a case of huddling close in order to find support against attacks from the outside.

The British actively furthered this difference by encouraging suspicion and mistrust between these communities through their policies and their public pronouncements.[2] The Afro-Guyanese moved to the urban centres looking for work, and so were more fully exposed to British culture, to the centres of power and to literacy. This relative urbanization, along with the Christianization of the community, aligned the Guyanese of African descent closer to the metropolitan way of life as opposed to the Indo-Guyanese community's jealous guarding of their religious and cultural practices (of Hinduism and Islam) that were native to the subcontinent. And thus, through this continued separation of cultures in the West Indian society, there grew the mutually reinforcing images of the recalcitrant and tradition-bound "coolie" versus the more upwardly mobile and Westernized Afro-Caribbean. The latter was seen as more amenable to the hybrid processes of modernity and of creolization than the former.

If, in the material world, the Indo-Guyanese are at one end of the spectrum from the Afro-Guyanese, they are more connected in Dabydeen's work. In *Slave Song*, the characters and their history are Indo-Caribbean, but the images and the title bespeak the African heritage. So too in *Turner*, for example, where the poet recreates the famous painting *Slave Ship* by J.M.W. Turner. This is a story of a group of African slaves who were jettisoned at sea for the sake of profit. Dabydeen reconstructs the story of the almost submerged African slave in Turner's painting but gives him a past that consciously echoes the Indo-Guyanese ancestry.

Dabydeen creates this confluence in *Turner* deliberately. In his interview with Chelva Kanaganayakam (1995, 28), he points out that "if you read the poem carefully, the landscape that the African imagines with a cow being central to it is an Indian village experience". So is the creation myth of Manu, an Indian myth, to which the poem alludes in the context of life in the African village. Manu, the soothsayer, "the source and future / Chronicles of our tribe" refers to the ancient Indian composite mythological character, the one who survived the great deluge, author of the religious text *Manusmriti* (Dabydeen 1994, 36). In the poem, Manu becomes the ancestor of the slaves and merges, more completely than any other image, the twin histories of African slavery and Indian indenture. He tears away the *jouti* necklace from his body and as each child gathers a handful of random beads, he warns:

> That in the future each must learn to live
> Beadless in a foreign land; or perish.
> Or each must learn to make new jouti,
> Arrange them by instinct, imagination, study
> And arbitrary choice into a pattern
> Pleasing to the self and to others
> Of the scattered tribe; or perish.
>
> (p. 36)

Dabydeen creates here not just a common ancestry for all the tribes in the ship; he also emphasizes the creative effort involved in such an endeavour and the amnesia that is part of the process. In the poem, the dispersal engendered in the remote past of the common tribe now necessitates a reinvention of the present for the slaves on the ship. It also justifies Dabydeen's poetic recreation of this composite history in his work. And by thus merging the two separate historical and cultural narratives, Dabydeen legitimizes the otherwise marginalized Indo-Caribbean community in Guyana: if they share the same historical oppression with the Afro-Caribbeans, and if they demonstrate the same resistance to colonization, then they cannot be logically sidelined in society.[3]

Creole (and English)

The use of Guyanese Creole in his writing is one of the important markers of this mixed identity that Dabydeen fosters in his work. The poems in *Slave Song* are essentially in Creole, with supporting translations and glosses; in *Coolie Odyssey*, there are several such poems interspersed with others written in Standard English; and in his novels, he always has elements of Creole in the mouths of his Guyanese or Caribbean characters. The presence of Creole in these works has been seen as a rebellion against metropolitan ways of the imperial English in Dabydeen's poems. But this crossing of boundaries that is effected through this employment of Creole is done on the home front in Guyana as well as across the seas in England. By using Creole to depict the lives of the indentured labourers from India, Dabydeen also intersects the social histories of the Indo-Guyanese and the Afro-Guyanese.

The Creole usage thus needs to be examined in the context of two settings: his early, rural Guyanese home and his current home in England. His Guyanese address declares its allegiance to the "Indian" population in Guyana, because of its rural location and its connection to the plantations. To live here meant that he was seen as illiterate, rural and "Indian", and therefore non-Guyanese. In England, where he lives now, he belongs to a community that is stereotyped as inferior to the British in intellect and in wealth because of its history of slavery and indenture. His use of Creole slips in between both these disputed identities and questions the boundaries of each. In the context of Guyana, this usage hybridizes the Guyanese labourer of Indian descent and reconnects her or him to the Guyanese colonial past and hence to the post-independence present. In the context of England, the usage of Creole solidifies the Caribbean identity of Dabydeen and merges it with other Afro-Caribbean histories of colonial takeover.

The origins of the word "Creole" are explained thus by Brathwaite (1971, xiv–xv): "The word ['Creole'] itself appears to have originated from a combination of the two Spanish words *crier* (to create, to imagine, to establish, to found, to settle) and *colono* (a colonialist, a founder, a settler) into *criollo*: a committed settler, one identified with the area of settlement, one native to the settlement though not ancestrally indigenous to it." This definition shows the integral connection between the language and the community; but in Guyana, "Creole" signifies a language as well as an ethnicity. That is, the language that is spoken in Guyana is the Guyanese Creole, and the common perception on the street is that the Afro-Guyanese are the Creoles. It is the African heritage of the Caribbean that tends to subsume, and frequently exclude, other ethnic communities in the Caribbean.[4]

Creole[5] is an exclusionary term in some respects because, in the Caribbean, even though it is a fluid category, it is always used to denote the Afro-Caribbean community and a certain sense of assimilation with the metropolitan culture.[6] Therefore, the Afro-Guyanese, who migrated to the urban areas after slavery was abolished, and who were more fluent in English because of their exposure to schooling and to urban locales, were the Creoles. The Indo-Guyanese indentured labourers, shipped to Guyana from some of the poorest regions in India, and who initially guarded their culture by insulating themselves from outside influences, were termed "Indians". In other words, the indentured labourers were given a name that had no roots in the country of their nationality.

Dabydeen's use of the Creole in his work refers to both the ethnic and the linguistic aspects of the term "Creole" and deliberately conjoins the two in his delineation of the Indo-Guyanese. In *Slave Song*, for instance, the first fourteen poems, spoken in Creole in the voices of various people on the plantations, evoke the harsh realities of indentured life in nineteenth-century Guyana. These poems also deliberately merge the histories of slave trade and indentured labour, histories of people who were removed and distinct from each other until they came to Guyana. Thus the poems creolize Indian history and the Indian community in Guyana.[7] The very title of the book, referring to slave history, conjures up notions of the Atlantic slave trade and the African ancestry of the Caribbean. But the poems themselves highlight the repeated blending of ethnic perceptions about the Indo-Guyanese in a manner that is not evident in the life on the street. In other words, they mix the racial heritages of the Indo- and the Afro-Guyanese in the poetry, when these communities are kept more or less separate, in terms of ancestry, significance and importance, in the imagination and the politics of the Guyanese.

A good example of such contestation is the poem titled "For Rohan Babulal Kanhai" from *Coolie Odyssey*. The narrator extols the cricketing prowess of the Guyanese-born batsman Kanhai and sees his success on the cricket field as a vindication of the reputation of the entire Indo-Guyanese ethnicity. As part of the West Indian team, Kanhai is seen as batting for, and bringing glory to, the West Indies against the colonizing England by appropriating their game to his own ends. But having penetrated the "national" team of the West Indies, and by being accepted as part of the national image of the Caribbean, Kanhai is also seen as the bulwark against the local political targeting of the Indo-Guyanese by the administration in the mid-1950s and the 1960s. His batting is seen in terms of the cane-cutting on the plantations:

> Kanhai
> Cutlass whack six,
> Leather ball red
> Like Whiteman restless eye.
> One ton cane-runs
> Cropped, all day in hot sun the man cut
> And drop on he back
> To hook two and lash four:
>
> (Dabydeen 1988, 22)

Kanhai dominates the cricket field unlike the exploited cane-cutters in their own field and thus reinstates their pride; their lashes are played out as his fine batting lashes at the colonizer's ball. And his establishment as a pre-eminent batsman of the West Indian team is seen as a vindication for the local identity of the Indo-Guyanese who were marginalized and brutalized by the ethnically divisive administration of Burnham:

> And Burnham blow down we house and pen
> Like fireball and hurricane
> And riverboat pack with crying and dead
> Like Old Days come back of lash and chain
> . . . and every ball blast
> Is cuff he cutting back for we,
> Driving sorrow to the boundary
>
> (Dabydeen 1988, 22)

Thus, Kanhai's batsmanship rewrites the story of the colonized on the field of the national game of England, and it also revises the notion of "Creole" and "Guyanese" in Guyana.

At the same time, Dabydeen's poetry is as concerned with the establishment of connections between the Guyanese and the British as it is with the erasure of the boundaries between the Indo-Guyanese and the Afro-Guyanese. The use of Creole indicates the poet's efforts to locate himself in the larger metropole of letters in England. After all, when Dabydeen wrote his first book, "[His] use of Creole in *Slave Song* was influenced not by living in a village in Guyana, but by being in a library in Cambridge where [he] was reading medieval alliterative verse" (Binder 1989, 70). Even as the use of the Creole penetrates the fractures of the local Guyanese society, this usage was as influenced by its contrary status to contemporary British English society as it was to local politics in Guyana.

Being Creole is identified with being "modern" because it indicates closeness with metropolitan culture in Guyana. Both in Guyana and in England, however, *speaking* or *writing* in Creole invites identification with the "native" as opposed to the cosmopolitan, the illiterate as opposed to the sophisticated, and the parochial as opposed to the global. As Shondel Nero observes, "Although the majority of the Caribbean people speak some form of English-based Creole, they continue to label their language as English, at least in public domains, for Creole is associated with low racial, social, political and economic status" (Nero 1997, 587). The descriptor "English" is thus used to imply sophistication and demonstrates an elevation of one's status to metropolitan ways.[8]

But Dabydeen harnesses this subtext of "rural" and "poor" of spoken Creole in a haunting manner in "Guyana Pastoral", from *Slave Song*. This poem refers to the Wismar killings of 1964, when the racial politics of the Burnhamite government resulted in violent clashes between the Guyanese of African and Indian origin, and several Indo-Guyanese women were raped and killed:

> Under de tambrin tree wheh de moon na glow
> Laang, laang, laang, she lay, laang, laang
> She cry, but de wind na blow
> An dem wraang an straang
> An dem wuk an dem bruk till fowlcack-crow.
> Who see who hear when she belly buss, when she mout
>   splash blood?
>
> Only de jumbie-umbrella dat poke up e white eye from de mud.
> (Dabydeen 2005, 21)

The tragedy of the rape and murder of the woman is underscored by the language used here. The short stresses of "wuk" and "bruk" in the fifth line, the harsh consonantal repetition of "k" and the simple sounding and unforgiving monosyllabic rhythm of the line all conspire to paint this already brutal depiction with a starkness that is shocking. And that blunt cruelty of the language ("belly buss") sets up a staggering contrast in the last line of that stanza, where the "jumbie umbrella" evokes several layers of connotations that interact in complex ways with the viciousness of the act described here. In his critical notes, Dabydeen tells us that the "jumbie umbrella[s]" are "white mushrooms that sprout overnight and are therefore thought of as ghostly things by the people; 'jumbie' means 'ghost' . . . " (p. 43). The horror arises because of the visual contrast of the soft, white, pure-looking mushrooms and the murdered woman whose "belly" is "buss"; also because the dead woman is almost fodder for the growing vegetation, the gruesome life growth on the body of the dead woman. And finally note the number of connotations that are collapsed in the word "jumbie". Before one gets the full meaning of the word from the notes, as an English reader, the image and sound of "jumbie umbrella" is almost cute; there is a sense of playfulness in this manner of looking at mushrooms as little white umbrellas of the forest. But in this line of the poem, the sense of innocence is taken further to indicate lush indiscriminate growth in nature; nature is seen as uncaring of the death of the girl as it continues to grow and multiply. And when we realize that "jumbie" refers to ghosts, it adds that additional aural image of the silence of the deep forests; the reader sees the visual image of utter abandonment and loneliness and the melting away of the material body.

One can find such instances in most of Dabydeen's work. But none of these works, poetry or prose, is entirely in Creole. *Slave Song* has fourteen initial poems in Creole, and these are surrounded by lengthy critical explanations in English, along with an easy-to-handle translation of the poems. In fact, the Creole poems come in an envelope of commentary by the poet as critic, the poet as translator and finally the poet as art historian. When the poet puts a Creole poem at the beginning of the text and the English translations and the glosses at the end of the book, he first legitimizes his Creole identity, then shows, through the subsequent translations, that he can use the Queen's English if he so wishes. The use of Creole then becomes an emphatic statement of a credo. He also forces the reader to encounter, handle and get acquainted with something that she or he would otherwise find alien and strange.

The reader can see this withholding of the meaning in the text in another way. The translations are really not the very best. Mark McWatt shows how the translations in *Slave Song* clean up and standardize or make acceptable what is individual or crude in Creole (McWatt 1994, 21–22). This standardization also makes them relatively ordinary. But this unsatisfactory translation is not because of Dabydeen's literary inability. The poet gives ample evidence of his mastery of form and language (both Creole and English) in all his books. For instance, Dabydeen speaks through Mungo, his narrator in the novel *A Harlot's Progress*, when he says contemptuously, "Put this down in your book, Mr Pringle, properise it in your best English" (Dabydeen 1999, 11). There is self-consciousness about the usage of the Creole that denies it the orientalized status of a naïve, simplistic reflection of the society of the indentured labourers. Earlier in the novel, Mungo says, "Pish! Where the bee sucks there suck I. Let me talk like dis and dat till the day come that I die, soon" (p. 5). This brief passage shows a knowledge of Shakespeare, the grasp of the literature and culture of England, the sophisticated juxtaposition of the Shakespearean line with his own Creole line, and his ability to make them rhyme (I/die), but also his refusal to do so completely by adding "soon" at the end of the line. It shows the narrator's guile in deliberately adopting the mask of the innocent native, and it shows Mungo's, and the writer's, scorn for the seemingly superior society's desperate need for voyeurism.

In addition, the Guyanese culture becomes equal to the actual past of English and European culture by this alignment of the Creole with Shakespearean writing. In Dabydeen's poetry, "primitive" Guyana thus becomes "ancient" Guyana, the precursor of modern-day England, and part of its ancestral history. As the poet asserts in many of his interviews, "You cannot be Guyanese without being British, and you cannot be British without being Guyanese or Caribbean" (Binder 1989, 165). At least on the page, the Creole and the English stand on equal footing, even if they are seen as superior or inferior in the material world. The page presents an ideological wish fulfilment, as it were.

Dabydeen's work thus demonstrates his effort to enfold his writing in layers of contradictions, which protect it from the covetous eyes of English or Western readers and keep intact the "El Dorado" of his culture and his life. As he says in the eponymous poem, of the labourer who dies of jaundice on the plantation:

> They bury him like treasure,
> The coolie who worked two shillings a day
> But kept his value from the overseer
>
>   (Dabydeen 1988, 15)

Slave Song is hemmed in by Dabydeen's English words: the detailed preface that explains the history of the region and also the poetry that follows; the critical glosses that analyse most of the major aspects of the Creole poems; the translations that render Creole into a passable but substandard English; and the illustrations, taken from colonial prints and engravings, that add yet another layer of connotations that collude and collide with those of the Creole poems. Moreover, in the latest edition of the book (2005), twenty years after the first publication, there is the poet's postscript in which he refuses to accept any of this as his own work, thus confounding the reader even further: "This thing of darkness I don't acknowledge as mine" (Dabydeen 2005, 67). It is as if the Creole poems are in an unassailable fortress of words that will not allow any singular meaning to escape them; after all, if even the poet himself disinherits this language and this world, who can truly reach it? In this cloistering of the Indo-Guyanese self in *Slave Song*, there is a paradoxical attempt to make it visible to the reader (and thus affirm its existence), but also an attempt to put it beyond the reach of the Western gaze (and make it inviolable). The book demonstrates the impossibility of an outsider's view achieving a complete understanding of the plantation life, of its people, of Guyana, of the poet.

This fusion of separate pasts is an attempt by Dabydeen to overcome, in the only way he can, the injuries of the past inflicted upon his community, his nation and his family. It is an endeavour (that is, of course, unsuccessful in the end) to create a home in his work that is *not* afflicted by the ethnic violence of his native Guyana. Even as he depicts the horror of the communal fights between Indo- and Afro-Guyanese, his poetry also expresses the hope that they will come together. Through the depiction of the abuse, he highlights the differences, but by merging the pasts, he tries to do on the page what is not yet achieved on the ground. This strategy also signals an effort to validate his Indo-Guyanese roots, because it gives their story the same authority and sanction that the narratives of the African slaves have had throughout history.

Finally, in the same process of rewriting the story of Guyana's past, Dabydeen also merges the histories of India and Guyana in his work. In his novel

The Counting House, the characters Vidia and Rohini speak Guyanese Creole in their native Indian village, even before they have stepped on to Guyanese shores. While the language appears odd and unfamiliar in the context of the Indian setting, Dabydeen manages to make Guyanese history part of the Indian landscape and culture in this manner. Dabydeen deliberately employs this in his attempt to obfuscate the linearity of history and the fait accompli of colonization. He erases the boundaries between Guyana and India on one side, and Guyana and England on the other.

The excitement in Dabydeen's work comes from the inability of the poet himself, and of the reader, to capture any unitary or singular meaning of his work. And in the end, the work seems to aim at a complex insubstantiality that emerges out of a frustrated inability to stake any one clear position on the issue of postcolonial identity.[9] When taken together with the repeated emphasis on images of impotence in his work, the reader begins to understand Dabydeen's yearning for such invisibility: "This is another aspect of creolization. I don't want to be 'authentic' about the African experience, nor do I want to be 'authentic' about the Indian experience, because I'm neither, because I'm both in a kind of a ghostly way" (Dawes 2001, 202). And in his interview with Döring and Härting, Dabydeen states this as an intentional effect of his work: "I like the idea of disappearance. The absolute absence of bodies . . . [which] emerges from a recognition that for black people, or for people from the colonies, your physique was yourself. Your existence was because of your physique: to cut cane . . . So therefore, what you really want to do now is not to write the body – because to write the body is to write those grievances . . . You are trying to escape from landscape, body, history" (Döring and Härting 1995, 40). This statement explains the disappearance of the body, even when it is so graphically presented in mutilated forms. The slave's body is racked and destroyed in *Slave Song*; Mala's raped and abused body cannot be found even by her own family; the child in the sea in *Turner* is an aborted foetus – Dabydeen's poetry presents many kinds of erasures.[10] But what makes this work more than the fudging of histories is the poet's anguished acknowledgement that this method of creating a new self in his poetry does not work.

The elision of identities for the sake of affirming the Indo-Guyanese community has now come full circle by moving towards an annihilation of *any* identifiable self. Nor is this disappearance affirmative; *Turner* ends with the poet's baleful cry of dispossession that lists the absences of everything that would root his self: landscape, religion, land, art and, finally, family and mother. Even while it signifies freedom, this seems suspiciously like a depletion of the speaker's life:

> No savannah, moon, gods, magicians
> To heal or curse, harvests, ceremonies,
> No men to plough, corn to fatten their herds,
> No stars, no land, no words, no community,
> No mother.
>
> (Dabydeen 1994, 40)

This is both a freeing experience and an experience of utter deprivation and loneliness. As the poet says,

> I wanted the Garden of Eden to be the sea, which has no landscape, no land, no nationality or ethnicity. A sea is a place of erasure. I wanted that to be the place where Adam would be born. It didn't work out that way. It was a stillborn child and a dead African in the poem. The sea becomes an empty Eden in the poem. (Kanaganayakam 1995, 29)

Because of such multiple layers of oppositions, his work also exudes a sense of imaginative exhilaration that is not easily explicable in the context of the depraved sexuality often present in the work. The reader navigates the liminal space of horror (at the depiction of the colonized life) and excitement (at the narrative and poetic experimentation in the work that always stops you from a transparent understanding of this colonized existence). As the poet says, this is his Eden, notwithstanding all losses: destruction translated as a sorrowful renewal.

Notes

1. For a closer look at the effect of such indenture policies on the gender discourse in Guyana and in the Caribbean, see Madhavi Kale (1998), Viranjini Munasinghe (2001), Patricia Mohammed (2003), Shalini Puri (2004), Aisha Khan (2004) and Brinda Mehta (2006).
2. See Madhavi Kale (1998).

3. See Viranjini Munasinghe for an ethnographic study of Indo-Trinidadians and how they construct their "Trininness" by resurrecting and asserting their Indian ancestry. While this study deals with Trinidad and not Guyana, the larger thesis has wider applicability with regard to the study of Indian indentured labour in the region.
4. See Frank Birbalsingh (1993) or Moore-Gilbert (1997, 195). For a discussion of how it is a well-established fact that "Creole" and "East Indian" are opposing and mutually exclusive categories in common parlance in Trinidad, see Viranjini Munasinghe (2006). Also, see Brinda Mehta (2006).
5. The term "Creole" includes French Creole in this context.
6. On the other hand, there is Maryse Condé, who objects to the effacement of the African element in Caribbean history by the emphasis on the Creole nature of the culture and language: "I have some problems with the term *créolité* because it makes us forget the African origins of Caribbean culture. With its accent on the fusion of multiple cultural elements, Africa becomes just another constitutive culture. But this does not do it justice in terms of the role Africa has played in Antillean history. It effaces the history of slavery, of the plantation culture, and the economic foundations of the island. The term *créolité* makes the cultural laboratory more important" (Apter 2001, 94).
7. Shalini Puri (2006, 219) uses the term "dougla poetics" to indicate this phenomenon, thus claiming a devalued racial term to highlight both the hybrid nature of such processes and also their dangerous forbidden nature: "Arising out of the Mauritian experience of Indian indentureship, Khal Torabully's conception of 'coolitude', like Singh's 'I am a Coolie' and my own arguments for a dougla poetics, revalues and appropriates a previously pejorative term."
8. See Drummond (1980) where he shows how "English" becomes a shifting descriptor that denotes diverse ethnic practices but connotes elite status.
9. This blending of pasts does not imply a disassociation from the material world or its harsh realities, even though such a position can be interpreted as such a disengagement. In his interview, Dabydeen ruefully confesses to Dawes (2001, 203): "you'll still be a Paki at a bus-stop in England, ten thugs around, and you're shit-scared because you don't have enough money for a taxi fare – you don't get away from these things. But I think in art anyway, I want to explore the possibilities of a total freedom from the social being."
10. See Döring (1998) for an extensive analysis of the figure of disappearance in Dabydeen's novels like *The Intended*.

References

Apter, E. 2001. "Crossover Texts/Creole Tongues: A Conversation with Maryse Condé". *Public Culture* 13, no. 1: 89–96.
Binder, W. 1989. "David Dabydeen". *Journal of West Indian Literature* 3, no. 2: 67–80.
Birbalsingh, F. 1993. *Indo Caribbean Resistance*. Toronto: TSAR.
Brathwaite, E. 1971. *The Development of Creole Society in Jamaica, 1770–1820*. Oxford: Clarendon.
Dabydeen, D. 1988. *Coolie Odyssey*. London: Hansib.
———. 1994. *Turner: New and Selected Poems*. London: Cape.
———. 1999. *A Harlot's Progress*. London: Vintage UK.
———. 2005. *Slave Song*. Leeds: Peepal Tree Press.
Dawes, K. 2001. "Interview with David Dabydeen". In *Talk Yuh Talk: Interviews with Anglophone Caribbean Poets*. Charlottesville, VA: University Press of Virginia.
Döring, T. 1998. "The Passage of the Eye/I: David Dabydeen, V.S. Naipaul and the Tombstones of Parabiography". In *Postcolonialism and Autobiography*, ed. A. Hornung and E. Ruhe, 149–66. Amsterdam: Rodopi.
Döring, T., and H. Härting. 1995. "Amphibian Hermaphrodites: A Dialogue with Marina Warner and David Dabydeen". *Third Text* 30: 3–45.
Drummond, L. 1980. "The Cultural Continuum: A Theory of Intersystems". *Man*, New Series 15, no. 2: 352–74.
Kale, M. 1998. *Fragments of Empire: Capital, Slavery and Indian Indentured Labour Migration in the British Caribbean*. Philadelphia: University Press of Pennsylvania.
Kanaganayakam, C. 1995. *Configurations of Exile: South Asian Writers and their World*. Toronto: TSAR.
McWatt, M. 1994. "His True-True Face: Masking and Revelation in David Dabydeen's *Slave Song*". In *The Art of David Dabydeen*, ed. K. Grant, 15–26. Leeds: Peepal Tree Press.
Mehta, B. 2006. "Engendering History: A Poetics of the Kala Pani in Ramabai Espinet's *The Swinging Bridge*". *Small Axe* 11, no. 1: 19–36.
Moore-Gilbert, B. 1997. *Postcolonial Theory: Contexts, Policies, Practices*. Montreal: Black Rose Books.
Munasinghe, V. 2001. *Callaloo or Tossed Salad? East Indians and the Cultural Politics of Identity in Trinidad*. Ithaca: Cornell University Press.
Puri, S. 2004. *The Caribbean Postcolonial: Social Equality, Post-Nationalism and Cultural Hybridity*. New York: Palgrave Macmillan.

CHAPTER 3

Fresh Names
Audience, Authenticity and the African Imaginary in *Turner* and *A Harlot's Progress*

NICOLE MATOS

"STILLBORN FROM ALL THE SIGNS" — this is the first sentence of David Dabydeen's *Turner* (2002, 9), and as its many commentators have noted, an opening that can be read ambiguously doubled: stillborn or born, still? But also intriguing, if less well discussed, is the doubled meaning that can be made to turn[1] on the phrase "from all the signs". The literal meaning, clearly, is "the infant shows all the features of stillbirth", but there's a second relevant transcription: "[something – the subject cagily absent] is stillborn from (due to, because of) all the signs." In part, this more linguistic, structuralist rendering suggests a meta-commentary on poetics to follow, as Heike Härting (2007, 57–58) describes: "The brokenness and silence of the phrase and image of the stillbirth contrasts with the abundance of signs and words, of language and representation . . . The double inscription of 'Still/born', then, indicates that Dabydeen's poem articulates identities through various histories, through a play of lack (stillbirth) and excess (multiplicity of signs)." But where Härting emphasizes "contrast", I might emphasize more doubleness or ambiguity – a reminder that textual "brokenness" can be a function of excess and abundance as often as silence or lack. Ultimately, both *Turner* and the closely linked *A Harlot's Progress* are deeply concerned with one locus of just this point: the manner in which narratives of Africa, of the Middle Passage and of slavery are stultified through excess, crushed and overburdened with preconceived signs, in the minds of many Western audiences.

Dabydeen's preface describes the ethos of *Turner* in terms reminiscent of many other Caribbean writers: "When [the narrator] awakens it can only partially recall the sources of its life, so it invents a body, a biography, and peoples an imagined landscape. Ultimately, however, the African rejects the fabrication of an idyllic past. His real desire is to begin anew in the sea but he is too trapped by grievous memory to escape history . . . The desire for transfiguration or newness or creative amnesia is frustrated" (2002, 7). Critics have long noted that this stance seems to parallel the "Adamic act of naming so prominent in Walcott, particularly in *Another Life*" (Burnett 1999, 19) or "Brathwaite's fascination with naming in *The Arrivants* . . . [names] retrieved through a journey back, through a journey to an existing origin" (Dawes 1997, 206). But the catalogues of *Turner* and *A Harlot's Progress*, their shared lexicon of specified flora and fauna, are neither exactly: not the "fresh names"[2] promised, which from the first are not new, nor originary retrieval of their narrators' authentic African memories. They are instead, I would argue, the canny anticipation and redirection of a certain sort of audience malfunction, a playful but pointed evocation of readers' own complicity in overdetermined modes of "exotic" representation.

Though the preface says little about the nature of *Turner*'s African imaginary ("Most of the names of birds, animals and fruit are made up"), this casual disavowal – suspiciously like Ruskin's "tossed overboard" footnote[3] – belies the texture evident in the actual poem. To take, for example, the first ten lines of the second section, is to identify already at least three different levels of invention:

> It [the stillborn infant] plopped into the water and soon swelled
> Like a brumplak seed that bursts buckshot
> From its pod, falling into the pond
> In the backdam of my mother's house, and fattening,
> Where small boys like I was hold sticks to the water
> For fish; branches strippled and shaped from the impala
> Tree, no other, for we know – only the gods
> Can tell how – that they bend so supple,
> Almost a circle without snapping, yet strong
> Enough to pull in a baby alligator.
>
> (Dabydeen 2002, 10)

However incredible-sounding, the biology of the "brumplak seed" is real enough; the plant seemingly referenced, *Hura crepitans*, is known throughout the Caribbean as monkey-pistol tree (Allsopp 1996, 486–87). Though "impala" inscribes a legitimate African animal, there's no such thing – at least none that I can find – as an "impala tree". Meanwhile, the poor "alligator" is seriously misplaced: though frequently confused with the African crocodile, alligators are native only to the Americas and Asia.[4] Add to this "backdam" – a uniquely Caribbean word, literally the dam that marks the outskirts of a sugar plantation, more generally a distant undeveloped piece of land (p. 59) – but a word unfamiliar enough to most non-Caribbean readers as to be taken (wrongly) as pure invention. What emerges is a deconstructive stratagem of quite devious complexity.

There are plenty of outright inventions, often in the modifier position of some otherwise commonplace noun phrase – "pakreet shell[s]" (Dabydeen 2002, 10), "barak shells" (p. 12), but also "cowrie shells" (p. 24), which just might be plausible. Fabricated "abara fruit" (p. 12) and "jilips" (p. 33) mingle with the more verifiable "yams" (p. 33) and "plantains" (p. 29), but also with dissonant geographical outliers – "tamarind" (p. 12) (possible, especially if the landscape is *East* Africa, but carrying much more prominent Caribbean and Indian associations) and "cacti" (p. 32) (indigenous only to the New World, and carrying associations as such[5]). Sometimes the same syllables repeat almost too often, as when a "chaltee tree" (p. 10) is followed by a "chaktee straw" (p. 11) and then by "mantee seeds" (p. 21): evidence of an exhausted imagination, or just common sound patterns in some honest foreign tongue? Like a scratch to an itch, the ghost of some English word will, from time to time, flit across the unfamiliar phonemes: "panoose" (p. 12) – papoose?; "hemlik" (p. 11) – hemlock? But the passing familiar is also passing strange, as such associations (the Algonquin? Socrates?) raise new incongruities of their own. "Blue aramantines" (p. 33) suggest an allusive anagram,[6] while a "daedal seed" startles in its arcane accuracy: intricate, multifaceted, worthy indeed of close examination:

> . . . I stare
> Into [the pond's] face as into a daedal
> Seed which Manu would hold up to the sky
> For portents of flood, famine, or the crop
> Of new births to supplement our tribe
>
> (p. 31)

More cruelly startling, among the false animals, the "straplee monkey" (p. 12), "jenti-cubs" and "harch" (p. 14), reference to "gannets" (p. 17): quite likely the sea-bird species picking the corpses in J.M.W. Turner's painting.

More relevant than this catalogue of heterogeneous specimens, of course, is a sense of their overall effect on a non-specialist reader. The text offers the option, on the one hand, of reading at the edge of one's ignorance, in a state of vigilance lest the distinction between the ethnographic real and imaginary erode any further. (How early was corn introduced to the African continent? Would a child of the "savannah" [p. 12] build a house on stilts, in the style of a flood plain? Are there any such foods as "ocho" and "sarabell" [p. 13]?) Or else it offers the option of allowing oneself to be swept along in a sort of surrendering monotony, registering each detail under empty sign of "the African": either option a self-implicating trap. Thus a potentially exoticizing semiotics, extant heuristically in the mind of the reader, is turned by Dabydeen to the purpose of *strategic* exoticism, defined by its "destabilizing effect on the readers it addresses": "First because it reminds these readers of their interpretive limits and of the inevitable biases behind their attempts to construct Africa as an object of cultural knowledge; second, because it redeploys the anthropological technique of participant-observation as the metaphor for a self-empowering, but also potentially self-incriminating, cultural voyeurism; and third, because it illustrates the 'epistemic violence' that underwrites the colonial encounter" (Huggan 2001, 56). Determinative control is wrestled from the audience back to the writer. The cow winks with a harlot's eye.[7] The figure of "ambush" (Dabydeen 2002, 11), of oblique attack, haunts the text at every turn.[8]

Turner's ambush of cunning, knowing creation is continued in *A Harlot's Progress,* but with the force of Dabydeen's critique refined and refocused. Dabydeen himself has spoken of *Turner* as a text in several ways "ghostly" – haunted by J.M.W. Turner's painting and by the dead of the Middle Passage, but also by a loose halo or aura of ironized authenticity: "The drowned man's landscape is ghostly and part of that ghostliness is the fabricated names of the fauna and the flora. This is another aspect of creolization: I do not want to be 'authentic' about the African experience nor do I want to be 'authentic' about the Indian experience, because I'm neither; but I'm both in a kind of ghostly way" (Dawes 1997, 206). One of the poem's most crucial ghosts is Olaudah Equiano, author of the popular eighteenth-century slave narrative. Dabydeen has made clear his special fascination with Equiano: "The writer who has really influenced me emotionally has been Equiano. Equiano is somebody who has definitely entered into my writing, almost like a posthumous spirit or a posthumous presence" (Stein 1999, 29).

Unaddressed (perhaps pointedly so) in Dabydeen's scholarship, but nonetheless relevant, is present-day controversy over Equiano's strict veracity. As Henry Louis Gates Jr (1988, 153), puts it, gently: "Equiano told a good story, and he even gives a believable account of cultural life among the Igbo peoples of what is now Nigeria . . . Like his friend Cugoano, Equiano was extraordinarily well read, and, like Cugoano, he borrowed freely from other texts." As Lars Eckstein quotes S.E. Ogude, more bluntly: "Much of Equiano's *Interesting Narrative* is pure fiction" (Eckstein 2006, 28).

But the truth of Equiano's life story, Eckstein among others suggests, is less important than what the quandary teaches us about the nature of his *Narrative,* and by extension, the whole slave narrative genre, as texts under enormous intentional and rhetorical strain. Bearing the weight of proof of their authors' very humanity, such writing required a near-virtuoso authorial performance, "a fragile 'balancing act' between a decidedly pragmatic component (which aims at selling the autobiography as much as possible and with the utmost political effect) and an expressive component (which aims at an affective truthfulness of adequate expression of the sufferings induced by slavery and racism) . . . an interplay between narrative strategies that appeal to and confront contemporary public taste and convictions and strategies that vouch for the authenticity and truthfulness of the account" (pp. 29–30). It is this tension, heightened to a ludic, hysterical crisis, that *A Harlot's Progress* develops as its major theme. Even more directly than the opening of *Turner*, the first scene of *A Harlot's Progress* stages questions of authenticity and audience; its exposition, in a present tense, rather like dramatic stage-directions:

> *22nd April 17*——. Mr Pringle sits at the table in Mungo's garret, a table which Mungo uses as a desk, a place to eat and a place to lay out the Bible. He shuffles his blank papers into a neat pile. He jabs the nib of his pen into the inkwell and stirs nervously, awaiting word . . .
>
> "Something must be said", Mr Pringle urges, "there must be a story." He withdraws his pen from the inkwell and looks at Mungo with a dog's imploring eyes.
>
> Mungo, master of the situation, squints at Mr Pringle, as if barely making out the shape of the younger man. He makes a heroic effort to lean his head in Mr Pringle's direction, groaning in the act. (Dabydeen 2000, 1)

Languid in his garret, Mungo is, on the one hand, the starving but empowered, even messianic ("awaiting word") artist; his former status as a slave now, ironically, the source of his value. Though Mungo is "master" of the moment, the mercantile underpinnings of his relation to white society has scarcely changed: a quid pro quo is demanded, and prefigured ominously (for one familiar with the insistent sexual politics to follow) in the shape of a transcriptional rape ("he jabs the pen into the inkwell . . . groaning in the act"). Mr Pringle's momentary subservience is coded in his "dog's imploring eyes"; but so, too, his inevitable dominance in a system of imagery – Hogarth's contemporaries[9] – where dog and black are considered a matched pair.

From here, *A Harlot's Progress* unfolds into the space triangulated by Mungo's resistance, Pringle's "hunge[r]" (p. 4) for Mungo's private story, and – least visibly, but perhaps most importantly – the unwittingly proscriptive expectations of even a benign abolitionist audience, already projecting the stereotypical prosaic and pious pursuits of ex-slavery ("a place to eat and a place to lay out his Bible") over the literal seat of the novel's quixotic art. The "slave narrative" that follows, ambiguously co-authored by Mungo and Pringle,[10] is a parodic stream of regurgitated textualisms: a send-up of everything from high modernism – "Pa is far. He is never here. He is never" (p. 11) – to negritude – "What is the katran bush? It is the sleep in my eyes. It is the white slick on the Afric's land" (p. 12) – to Amerindian myth[11] – "Legend tells of a band of marauders, cubbed of the moon, rough-faced and pallid . . . Our tribe scurried from the dreadful white light of their presence. We sought shelter in deep caves. We daubed mud over our bodies to create a cloak of invisibility. Still the light reached us, bathing sperm and womb, so that our tribe dwindled to a few. In desperation we ventured out to shoot arrows to the moon" (p. 33) – to *Heart of Darkness* and Afrocentrist[12] history:

> It was the bush which altered the Greek mind, the colossal squalor of it . . . It was the bush – its insects, its animals, its rank vegetation, its baneful noises, its human eyes gleaming from behind dense foliage – which drove the Greeks to massacre. . .
> They painted, they philosophized. They engaged in speculations on geometry. They measured the relationship between shapes and planes. They codified these in an abstruse algebra. And all this civilization they bestowed unto their brightest slaves and mulatto offsprings. (pp. 31–32)

Where other slave narratives might "borrow", Mungo's steals wildly and anachronistically. Where other slave narratives might stretch the truth, Mungo's is, from its cover forward, hopelessly fractured: "Dabydeen suggests, even in the design of the first edition, that his story is inevitably 'broken'. The paperback cover is unevenly laminated to imitate broken glass, but so convincingly that the book looks damaged. (I put the first copy in the pile back, thinking I could remedy the situation)" (Wallace 2000, 239).

Like Pringle, who demands "an epic, the frame of which he has already constructed in his mind" (Dabydeen 2000, 6), we readers have, Dabydeen implies, deeply embedded assumptions about the proper way Mungo's story should unfold. It might begin with an anthropological excursion into tribal culture, complete with exotic accoutrements: the "katran bush" (p. 17), "ocho and sarabell" (p. 18), and a cascade of other *Turner* favourites make a triumphant reappearance. It might portray kinship rituals – "Now I remember when my father died, but not how. It was beautiful. All the women went to the chatree hut in the middle of our village and danced all night. There men usually stayed, smoking, wrapping wounds, picking chigoes from their feet, feeding the fire, arguing, sometimes fighting over the last mouthful of changa-wine left in the pan" (p. 15) – deadly taboos – "The Headman brands my forehead with the sign of evil, and I am put into a deep hole which my mother is made to dig, and she surrenders me to it with her own hands, for my disobedience has brought sin upon her and the threat of destruction to our village, for our ancestors have departed in anger from the katran bush, leaving us no defense against enemies of flies, drought, malicious stars, tribes with different scars" (p. 20) – and precocious, primal sexuality: "A jungle of breast is offered me, for tonight, only tonight, my father dead, all the women are my wives, by antique custom. I can choose to hunt the young gazelle or the red-lipped snake. The women stamp their feet around me, and drink and drink. They shudder and fall to the ground, pretending to be slain beasts" (p. 15).

As Mungo puts it, mock-innocently, "your normal naked savage" (p. 41), your "normal malnourished child existing on an African diet of animal droppings" (p. 27). Of the slave ship, the usual tropes are present: the smells – "I will not dwell on the sudden effluvium of air that greeted us when the hatch was lifted, for there is ample appeal to your nostrils in Abolition literature written by Englishmen truly appalled by the foulness of the African trade. Suffice it to say that even the olfactory gifts of Messrs Gay and Pope, in describing London's sewers, would be paupered by the stink of nigger-sweat" (p. 57) –

the casually grotesque violence and deaths – "When the ship pitched in a sudden rough sea, the chains tightened and cracked their ankles, spines and elbow joints. Sometimes arms and legs wrenched clean off, and their torsos rolled freely about the ship . . . One woman, torn from her chains, sans head and feet, rolled endlessly about, according to the rhythm of the waves battering the ship" (p. 49) – and the rationalizing comforts of Christian conversion: "I consumed the Eucharist on board and came to the knowledge that our true slavery was temporary slavery to death, our truth freedom the acquisition of a soul manacled eternally to the will of God. My Negro brethren below deck wrapped in chains and floating in their own faeces were in temporary distress" (p. 51). But all are tuned to a shrillness where the terrible becomes the ridiculous, and where our own readerly expectations, vicarious and voyeuristic, can no longer be denied.

Dabydeen's "fresh names", then, are ultimately "fresh" in a quite aggressive, performative and interactive sense. As "techniques of opacity" – in Aleid Fokkema's memorable Glissantian coinage (2007, 29) – that unbalance the reader, they evoke and thus paradoxically resist the "uninformed familiarity" at the centre of exoticist perception: "The exotic is not, as is often supposed, an inherent *quality* to be found 'in' certain people, distinctive objects or specific places: exoticism describes, rather, a particular mode of aesthetic *perception* – one which renders people, objects and places strange even as it domesticates them, and which effectively manufactures otherness even as it claims to surrender to its immanent mystery . . . a kind of semiotic circuit that oscillates between the opposite poles of strangeness and uninformed familiarity" (Huggan 2001, 13). Unwarranted and unearned (half-) familiars, they haunt Dabydeen's work to remind us of our own tendencies towards "ghost-writing" and that the most authentic longing of the exoticized other – "Each secretly longs for the familiarity of their ordinariness, instead of the artifice . . . made of their lives" (Dabydeen 2000, 97–98) – is simply beyond the power of our shared narrative to provide.

Notes

1. This trope spins busily: title of the poem and collection, it names also J.M.W. Turner, the slave-ship captain, *and* the stillborn infant.
2. What was deemed mere food for sharks will become
   My fable. I named it Turner.
   As I have given fresh names to birds and fish
   And humankind, all things living but unknown,
   Dimly recalled, or dead.
   (Dabydeen 2002, 9)
3. *Turner's* inspiration is, of course, J.M.W. Turner's *Slavers Throwing Overboard the Dead and Dying* (1840) and Ruskin's subsequent exegesis. Praising the painting's colour and composition, Ruskin refers to its subject only in a footnote: "She is a slaver, throwing her slaves overboard. The near sea is encumbered with corpses" (Ward 2007, 48). This gesture is akin, Dabydeen writes, to "something tossed overboard" (Dabydeen 2002, 7).
4. This might include, loosely, the four species of caiman native to Guyana; all are part of the subfamily Alligatorinae ("Black caiman" 2004).
5. African succulents "are often confused with cacti, but are very different plants. Cacti are exclusive to the New World where they did not evolve into the family Cactaceae until millennia after the Gondwanaland break-up" (Gilmer 2001). Few readers would be sure of that distinction without recourse to an encyclopedia or botanist, but that's exactly my point: the way these discrepancies launch a stealthy poetics of readerly self-doubt.
6. For "amarant[h]ine" – the "fadeless flower".
7. "So the cow stands still, / But looks at us with a harlot's eye and winks, / And we can see the mischief in its face" (Dabydeen 2002, 11).
8. See also, for example, "In the bush, special trees we climb to scout / For enemies, whom we will startle / With a torrent of twigs and fruit" (p. 18).
9. Dabydeen's brilliant reading of these and other aspects of eighteenth-century racial aesthetics are offered in *Hogarth's Blacks: Images of Blacks in Eighteenth Century English Art* (1987).
10. Though it is possible that the story that follows is Mungo's alone, the opening foregrounds Pringle's amanuensis. We cannot be sure whether the novel is a representation of Mungo's inner consciousness, Mungo's acquiescing verbal narration, Pringle's transcripts or some unholy marriage of all of these.
11. Shooting arrows to form a ladder to the moon is presented as an Amerindian creation myth in the fiction of fellow Guyanese writers Wilson Harris and Pauline Melville; Dabydeen tips his hat to these writers in his acknowledgements (Dabydeen 2000, 282).

12. Specifically, here, the Afrocentrist contention that much of Greek culture and philosophy was African-derived.

References

Allsopp, R. 1996. *Dictionary of Caribbean English Usage.* New York: Oxford University Press.
"Black caiman, prehistoric top predator". 2004. Iwokrama International Centre for Rain Forest Conservation and Development: http://www.iwokrama.org/forest/animals/blackcaiman.htm (accessed 2 November 2010).
Burnett, P. 1999. "Where Else to Row, but Backward?: Addressing Caribbean Futures through Re-visions of the Past". *ARIEL: A Review of International English Literature* 30, no. 1: 11–37.
Dabydeen, D. 1987. *Hogarth's Blacks: Images of Blacks in Eighteenth Century English Art.* Manchester: Manchester University Press.
———. 2000. *A Harlot's Progress.* New York: Vintage.
———. 2002. *Turner: New and Selected Poems.* Leeds: Peepal Tree Press.
Dawes, K. 1997. "Interview with David Dabydeen". In *The Art of David Dabydeen,* ed. K. Grant, 199–221. Leeds: Peepal Tree Press.
Eckstein, L. 2006. *Re-membering the Black Atlantic: On the Poetics and Politics of Literary Memory.* Amsterdam: Rodopi.
Fokkema, A. 2007. "Caribbean Sublime: Transporting the Slave, Transporting the Spirit". In *No Land, No Mother: Essays on the Work of David Dabydeen,* ed. K. Karran and L. Macedo, 17–31. Leeds: Peepal Tree Press.
Gates, H.L., Jr. 1988. *The Signifying Monkey: A Theory of African-American Literary Criticism.* New York: Oxford University Press.
Gilmer, M. 2001. *Euphorbia: A Hardy Plant Group from Africa.* Cactus and Succulent Society of America: http://www.cssainc.org (accessed 20 September 2009).
Härting, H.H. 2007. "Painting, Perversion, and the Politics of Cultural Transfiguration in David Dabydeen's *Turner*". In *No Land, No Mother: Essays on the Work of David Dabydeen,* ed. K. Karran and L. Macedo, 48–85. Leeds: Peepal Tree Press.
Huggan, G. 2001. *The Postcolonial Exotic: Marketing the Margins.* London: Routledge.
Stein, M. 1999. "David Dabydeen Talks to Mark Stein". *Wasafiri* 29: 27–29.
Wallace, E. K. 2000. "Telling Untold Stories: Philippa Gregory's *A Respectable Trade* and David Dabydeen's *A Harlot's Progress*". *Novel: A Forum on Fiction* 33, no. 2: 235–52.
Ward, A. 2007. "'Words Are All I Have Left of My Eyes": Blinded by the Past in J.M. Turner's *Slavers Throwing Overboard the Dead and Dying* and David Dabydeen's *Turner*". *Journal of Commonwealth Literature* 42, no. 1: 47–58.

Part 2

(RE)READING THE NOVELS

CHAPTER 4

Translating *The Intended*

JENNY DE SALVO

WHEN I FIRST BEGAN WORK ON the translation of *The Intended* (2005), I was clear about the *skopos* (Vermeer 1989, 227) that I wanted to pursue: to give David Dabydeen an Italian voice and to make him speak to the Italian reader in his own words. If it were possible to define *The Intended* with one word, I would say that it is a very balanced novel, constructed by the author in such a way that the reader is rarely overburdened, even when the mix between intertextuality and the various languages could, perhaps, be somewhat confusing. For the Italian translator, maintaining such a balance is not an easy task, and the dilemma of faithfulness is always at stake because, as Maria Tymoczko states, "no text can ever be fully translated in all its aspects: perfect homology is impossible between the translation and source. Choices must be made by the translator; there are admissions and omissions in the process, no matter how skilled the translator" (Tymoczko 1999, 23). The risks in any translation are always high and the *deforming tendencies* as outlined by Berman[1] (1985, in Venuti 2000, 280) always lie in wait. For example, it was important to be especially careful with the punctuation, because my spontaneous tendency was to respect the Italian punctuation system, especially the use of commas, and this risked breaking the rhythm of Dabydeen's narration.

After having read the book several times, I identified three central issues about this translation that I felt were essential to the ways in which I would deal with this text. The first was intertextuality. In *The Intended* two main kinds of intertextuality can be detected: apart from numerous references to English classical authors (Wordsworth, Blake, Chaucer, Milton), Dabydeen also borrows from and transforms Joseph Conrad's *Heart of Darkness* (1899).

The second and most challenging issue was the variety of registers and languages that Dabydeen's characters use throughout the novel. Borrowing from the character Shaz's statement that "black people have to have their own words" (Dabydeen 2005, 107), each of Dabydeen's characters appears to speak his own words depending on who she or he is; on who she or he was; and on where she or he came from.

The third issue – a somewhat open one – concerns the way in which the title is translated. Before analysing the ways in which I dealt with these issues, I should emphasize that in my own idea of translation "the Foreigner has to be welcomed as Foreigner" (Berman 1985, in Venuti 2000, 277), and not changed into some kind of "fuzzy" Italian. In addition, the reader has to be taken to the text and not vice versa.

1

In *The Intended,* references and allusions to other literary texts and, in particular, to texts of the English canon play a significant role. Sometimes their presence is overt and at other times they can only be detected through close and careful reading. In this section I begin by analysing some of the key references to the literary canon that can be found in *The Intended,* the particular use of which illustrates the subversive nature of Dabydeen's writing. I then focus my attention on the different strategies which could be adopted to deal with these references, and itemize those which I deemed as most suitable in achieving a result that would be comparable with the source text.

The first reference to an English canonical text is in the title itself, which alludes to the white female fiancée of Kurtz in Joseph Conrad's *Heart of Darkness.* Since Dabydeen's novel is involved in some form of postcolonial rewriting of Conrad's text, both in its subject matter and through its narrative structure, aspects of *The Intended* and *Heart of Darkness* are compared in detail in section 2 of this chapter.

The first explicit encounter with the English canon is found when the schoolmates take their English GCE examinations. While preparing for the exams, Patel seeks the help of his uncle, who writes for him "two long descriptive passages [that] were gorged with sweetmeats selected from *Roget's Thesaurus . . .* all Patel had to do was to memorize the two passages" (Dabydeen 2005, 12). Upon entering the room, while everyone else is nervous about the exam, it is Patel who is "swishing with confidence", sits down and starts to fill the page: "its emotion recollected in the tranquillity of the examination room". This last sentence is one of many covert references that the careful reader can find in the book, recalling the famous definition of poetry given by Wordsworth in his preface to *Lyrical Ballads* (1798): "Poetry is the spontaneous overflow of powerful feelings: it takes its origin from emotion recollected in tranquillity."

The result of this juxtapositioning between the "father" of English Romanticism, who recollects his inner emotions that will be read for centuries, with the figure of the fair-skinned Patel, who simply memorizes two passages without even knowing what he is writing about, is both irreverent and ironic at the same time. The situation becomes even more paradoxical when Patel turns the examination sheet and finds the words "Tiger! Tiger! Burning bright / in the forest of the night".

After writing the beginning of his essay, Patel turns to the title again: "In the forest in the *night* . . . fuck! they wanted the tiger described in the night time, whereas he had begun his essay in daylight" (p. 13). After being seized by panic for a moment, he finds the only solution is to reverse the story contained in his essay – an Indian story about a tiger kidnapping an Indian village baby – by making it begin in the night and finish in daylight. It is never mentioned that the title of the essay contains the first two verses of Blake's poem "The Tyger" (1794), one of the most anthologized poems in the English language. In this passage, Dabydeen's desecration of the English canonical text is total.

One of the central issues here is something that does not specifically concern translation in its strict literal sense, because from a linguistic point of view the translator's task is effortless, since both Wordsworth and Blake are published in Italian with official translations. Hence it would be sufficient to resort to the Italian version and simply insert this into the translation of *The Intended*. But, as we have seen, Dabydeen *uses* these two references in a very specific context, in order to create an ironic and paradoxical situation, and this must remain so in the target text as well.

As the primary reader of the source text, I asked myself if, without the aid of research undertaken before commencing the translation, I would have been aware of where these references originated. I therefore conducted a short survey

– a common translation practice – by asking friends and colleagues if they would have noticed these references, and the answer from most of them was "no". This reinforced my belief that translation by itself was not the right strategy in dealing with these references, and therefore I had to find a way to give the reader a hint that something more notable lay in those particular sentences. My options were as follows:

1. Leave the English version. I did not consider this a suitable strategy, first because an Italian translation of Wordsworth and Blake already exists, and these authors are studied in English literature courses held in Italian high schools. Second, leaving the sentences in their source language, on a page that is otherwise written in Italian and where it is stated that the schoolmates are taking their English GCE examination, could make an Italian reader think that the characters were facing a foreign language examination.

2. Apply the "adaptation" translation technique as outlined by Vinay and Darbelnet (1959, cited in Fawcett 1997, 39), thus changing the source content to conform to the target culture; that is, substituting the original verses with others from a recognizable Italian source. Blake's verses could, for instance, be substituted with Alessandro Manzoni's opening verses of his poem *Il Cinque Maggio,* which is one of the most famous Italian poems of the nineteenth century. Adaptation is, however, a high-risk strategy which can lead to what Levy calls "localization and topicalization" (1969, cited in Fawcett 1997, 40). An Italian reader might not only think that Italian literature is studied in English high schools, but that Manzoni is used for an English examination, and this is obviously nonsense. As far as Dabydeen's novel is concerned, therefore, I dismissed adaptation as a suitable option for translation.

In addition to the official translation, footnotes could be used to explain the references made by the author to classical English texts. This is, perhaps, the most reasonable option, but it would be a case in which the text is taken to the reader and, as I stated from the very beginning, this was not my idea of how this translation should work.

To place the Italian translation in italics: this was the strategy I adopted to signal to the reader that he or she is looking at a quotation. My assumption was that any reader of Dabydeen's fiction would be someone with a curious mind who would probably search the Internet to find out more about the source.

2

As far as the explicit references to Joseph Conrad's *Heart of Darkness* are concerned, no real problems arise when considering how to translate them. These references are overt, because the main protagonists in Dabydeen's novel are studying the Conradian text, and it provides the focus of some of the most interesting dialogues between the protagonist and Joseph, his Rastafarian friend. My aim in this section is, therefore, to compare the structure of *The Intended* with that of *Heart of Darkness*, insofar as both are works about journeys.

In *Heart of Darkness*, Marlow's tale "appears to be a single account of his journey" (Farn 2005, 32), yet it really contains several different ways of "perceiving a journey". Colonial travellers were sometimes motivated by the desire to improve the lives of the colonized, or in other instances impelled by the desire for monetary gain; while the journey itself can also be a path for initiation and emotional maturing (pp. 32–34).

Dabydeen's narrator can also be seen as undertaking a four-fold voyage, as outlined by Deandrea in his *Rewriting/Reprising* (2006), closely followed by the reader. The first of these "journeys" is the voyage into the heart of sexuality: from the very onset of the novel to its concluding paragraphs, the reader is able to follow the narrator's sexual and sentimental maturation. Sex is described as an "unknown darkness" and "the first automatic reaction to the darkness is to cough, as if to locate your body, to ensure that it came with you and was not left abandoned" (Dabydeen 2005, 10). In this passage, from the semantic point of view, the reader can find echoes of the unknown darkness located in *Heart of Darkness*. As she or he reads the description of a body in an uncomfortable position located in a reality that it really doesn't know, parallels can be drawn with the image of a migrant who arrives for the first time in an unknown land.

The second voyage made by the narrator is the one to the heart of London. The city in which the protagonists live is violent, and is used by Dabydeen as a paradigm for English and western societies in general. "Everything in this country is about money" (p. 128) says Shaz; it is a place "where people cared nothing for family, dumping their parents in old people's home, marrying and breeding and divorcing and bequeathing the children to the welfare, abusing their own kids or abducting other people's" (p. 19). In the kind of European society that is portrayed in Dabydeen's novel, the reader finds all of the vices which Dante described in his *Inferno*. The narrator's journey in *The Intended* parallels Marlow's journey in Conrad's *Heart of Darkness*, which, in turn, parallels Dante's descent into hell.

The third voyage is that from periphery to centre, in which the narrator's memories of Guyana are depicted as "a rural society which envisions England as a sort of myth, an idealized promised land" (Deandrea 2006, 5). What emerges from the narrator's flashbacks to his childhood in Guyana is an innocent attitude of respect and esteem for the white colonizers. In one passage that is set in Guyana during the Independence struggles, the protagonist recalls white people giving to children "nice free food and drinks . . . It was as if we were special children and the white people had come from far away to give us a treat". However, when he asks to his mother "Why white people giving we so much food?" she ironically replies: "Because they good, kind people, not nasty and stupid like we colonial trash. Is great curse will come on this country if the white people pack up and go" (Dabydeen 2005, 92).

The fourth type of voyage undertaken by the narrator is one in which he ventures an "exploration of the British model by the way of literature" (Deandrea 2006, 5). The study of literature appears to be the only form of redemption that the narrator can imagine; it is what will make him a civilized being, and what will allow him to be with his girlfriend Janet: "I will have become somebody definite, my education compensating for my colour in the eyes of her parents" (Dabydeen 2005, 173).

3

The Intended is a novel in which various forms of language have been used by the author for very specific purposes. It is possible to identify four different types of language: the Standard English spoken by the narrator; the broken English spoken by the migrants (Nasim's mother and Mr Ali); the Creole spoken by the young narrator and his friends in Guyana; and the patois spoken by the Rastafarian Joseph. Such a mixture provides a major challenge for the translator, who has to decide how to characterize each of these languages, without ignoring the differences and, at the same time, remaining aware that the risk of ridicule is always present. For each of these I will now outline the key problems that arise for an Italian translator, the different types of strategy that could be applied and the reasons for the choices I subsequently made.

A. Standard English

My analysis begins by focusing on two particular passages from Dabydeen's *The Intended*, designed to illustrate the type of questions that can arise in translating this aspect of the novel. In the first, while the protagonist and his friend Shaz are looking at advertisements to rent a house, they find one that states:

> Black beauty offers VIP massage to kind gents in comfort of her own house. Cleanliness assured and demanded (p. 68).

> *Bellezza di colore offre massaggi VIP a uomini generosi nel confort della sua casa. Igiene assicurata e richiesta.*

This is a short text with two *double entendres*: "VIP massage" and "kind gents". With the former, it gives the malicious idea of something that is far more than a massage, and a similar level of malice is obtained with the Italian formula "*Massaggi VIP*" which is a literal translation of the source text. As to "kind gents", the reference is to men who will be generous with their money (rich), and a literal translation would not work. "*Uomini gentili*" would sound like "kind men" and this is not the covert meaning; "*gentiluomini generosi*" would transmit the meaning but would also sound cacophonous. I opted for "*uomini generosi*" that is "generous men": I felt it was necessary to make explicit in Italian what was implicit in the source text; applying what Berman calls *clarification* (1985, in Venuti 2000, 280).

The second matter I want to consider in this section is the translation of what may be termed "word games", which are used by Dabydeen throughout the novel. In one passage, Joseph asks why Conrad named his characters Marlow and Kurtz. Shaz, who cannot understand Joseph's argument, answers in a sarcastic way that

"Mar" was an anagram of "ram" and "low" of "owl". Marlow was a ram like a battering ram . . . and like an owl because he refused to dream . . . As to Kurtz, well he was a cur, a human beast. (Dabydeen 2005, 75)

"Mar" era un anagramma di "ram", **ariete***, e "low" di "owl",* **gufo***. Marlow era un ariete perché era ostinato come un ariete da guerra . . . ed era come un gufo perché si rifiutava di sognare. Per quel che riguarda Kurtz, era un "cur",* **un cagnaccio***, una bestia umana.*

The choice of translation here was essentially unavoidable: I left in the English words and put the Italian version into (bold) italics.

B. The Language of the Migrants

This form of language is represented by the speech of Nasim's mother and Mr Ali. They both speak a broken form of English, which can be compared to the type of Italian spoken by migrants in Italy. To translate the passages in which Nasim's mother and Mr Ali spoke, I therefore used as a guideline *Italiano di Stranieri* (Giacalone 1973), in which a detailed analysis of the Italian language as spoken by migrants is provided. From Giacalone's research it emerges that

1. The syntax of migrants is guided by pragmatism; the verb is often used in the third singular person, while the use of the infinitive is not common.
2. The migrants have no major challenges in following the word order in sentences.
3. In the Italian language, words change regarding number and gender: the migrants quickly learn how to manage the number issue rather than that of gender.

Furthermore, I drew upon my own experience of teaching Italian to migrants, because there are two Pakistani students in my class who always make the same errors when they speak Italian. This is due to the fact that they still translate from their mother tongue to Italian, and this was helpful in understanding the differences between the structure of their source language and Italian.

With these ideas in mind I translated the speech of Nasim's mother and Mr Ali into a simple language, a basic register where the verb is always in the third person singular. Some examples will help to illustrate the method used:

> So nice you come see Nasim . . . you Nasim good friend, Nasim lucky. (Dabydeen 2005, 21)
>
> *Così bello tu viene vedere Nasim . . . Tu Nasim buono amico, Nasim fortunato.*

As in the source text, the first part of the sentence lacks the preposition after the verb (you come *to* see/*tu viene a vedere*) and the second part of the sentence lacks the verb (to be/*essere*), while the order of the adjectives (good/lucky/*buono*/*fortunate*) is correct. The differences are in the first part of the sentence, where the Italian version has more grammatical errors: this is due to the fact that in Italian the verb has to be conjugated. Hence, in the target text, beside the correct personal pronoun – the second singular person (*tu*/you) – we find the verb is actually conjugated as the third person singular *(viene* instead of *vieni).*

> Nasim go Sheffield soon. Good for him, no? Balham too-too nasty place. (p. 22)
>
> *Nasim andare Sheffield presto. Buono per lui, no? Balham troppo troppo posto cattivo.*

What is noteworthy in this second example is that, contrary to what has been stated above about the uncommon use of the infinitive by migrants in Italy, in translating the first sentence I used the infinitive. This is because the verb to go in Italian is the irregular *"andare"* that changes completely when it is conjugated.[2] The use of this verb is one of the most challenging for migrants in Italy and it would have been unlikely to find a woman that had just arrived in this country being able to use this verb in the right form. Hence, while both in the source text and in the target text it lacks the preposition, in the first we find a verb conjugated in the wrong form and in the second we find the verb in its infinitive form.

> Room to lett big house going cheap for person working 6727067 anytime or call round, 296 Cherry Road, anytime. (p. 69)
>
> *Stansa afito casa grande per poco a persona lavoratore 6727067 sempre o passare, 296 Cherry Road, sempre.*

In this final example, orthographic errors occur both in the source text and in the target text. In the Italian, *"stanza"* becomes *"stansa"*, which plays with the different sound of the two consonants, something that is very difficult for migrants to catch, and furthermore the double "f" and "t" in "*affitto*" (to rent) are ignored. In the target text we also find a *double entendre* that is not present in the source text, concerning the translation of "going cheape". The Italian equivalent of cheap is "*economico*", but it is unlikely that a migrant would use the adjective "*economico*"; also, in everyday spoken Italian it would not usually be said that something was "*economico*". If someone was saying they had bought something cheap, they would say they bought something "*per poco*", that is, at a relatively low price. The same "*per poco*" would also be used if it meant that a house could be rented for a short period of time. This is where the *double entendre* can be found in the target text: I made the assumption that whoever wrote the advertisement was clear about what they meant, and had used everyday spoken language while ignoring the ambiguous result.

C. Creole

Postcolonial writers often use Creole languages to distinguish some of their characters, yet in *The Intended* Dabydeen uses Creole only for the passages set in Guyana. The difficulties with translating Creole arise "from the absence in the target language of a sub-code equivalent to the one used by the source text in its reproduction of the source language" (Brisset 1990/1996, in Venuti 2000, 338). Creole is mainly characterized by its orthographic deviation from Standard English; therefore the translator has to make a choice about how to reproduce this singularity, and can either ignore the orthographic deviation and translate as if he or she were translating from Standard English, or use an Italian with orthographic deviations. I decided to ignore the orthographic deviation and to translate by lowering the register and inserting some colloquial forms. My reasoning was that an Italian reader who finds a book written in "broken Italian" could suddenly think that the person who is talking is an illiterate. Of course, Creole is not necessarily the language of illiterate Guyanese, and those who speak it are not deviating from their original tongue or making any kind of linguistic mistake, so it would have not only been unfaithful but also disrespectful to give an Italian reader the idea of Creole being a "second order language".

> Eh! Eh! You bring de chile wid you . . . and how is de Lord looking after you?
>
> Eh! Eh! *Ti sei portato dietro il ragazzo* . . . *e dimmi*, il Signore si prende cura di te?

But you must tek education . . . you hear . . . and pass plenty exam and work hard and get good job. (Dabydeen 2005, 31)

*Devi studiare . . . mi senti . . . e **vedi di** passare tutti **quegli** esami e di lavorare duro e di trovare un buon lavoro.*

In the examples above I have used bold italics for the colloquial Italian form. This strategy is now commonplace in Italy, but in the 1960s things were very different. For example, an Italian translation was made of Cyprian Ekwensi's novel *Jagua Nana* (1961), where the protagonist is a pidgin-speaking Nigerian woman. Just one example can illustrate the kind of the shift that occurred then, and is still ongoing in Italian translation practices today.

You no like my dress? . . . you vex wit' me . . . I know das wat you goin' to say. But speak true, dis be naked? (Ekwensi 1961a, 7)

Tu non piace mio vestito? . . . tu arrabbiato con me? . . . Io già sa cosa tu vuol dire. Ma parla con verità, questo essere nuda? (Ekwensi 1961b, 4)

In the target language the result trivializes the character: the woman who is speaking sounds not as a native speaker should, but like someone who is learning Italian with an awful teacher: neither the grammar nor the syntax is correct. In 1993, the novel was retranslated and republished with the following result:

Non ti va come sono vestita? . . . Sapevo che me lo dicevi. Ma dì la verità, ti sembro forse nuda? (Ekwensi 1993, 6)

The new translator opted for the strategy of lowering the register and used the colloquial form; at the same time the editor chose to use italics to mark the Italian colloquial form for pidgin.

The same strategy has been used in the translation of Biyi Bandele's first novel *The Sympathetic Undertaker and Other Dreams* (1991), which is characterized by a mixture of Standard English, Nigerian English and pidgin. The last is frequently used by the author when the protagonist Rayo writes down his notes, which are mostly connected with daily life. In the Italian translation the strategy is that of lowering the register and using everyday colloquial forms. Here also the publisher chose to differentiate these "notes" from the rest of the novel, by using a different font that is reminiscent of an old typewriter.

"E fit no be gunshot" I offered

"If that one no be gunshot" said the driver authoritatively "then this car when dey drive na Lizard" (Bandele 1991, 79)

"*Non sarà mica stato uno sparo*" *ho buttato lì*

"*Se quello non era uno sparo*" *ha detto l'autista con tono esperto* "*allora sono al volante di una lucertola*" (Bandele 2007, 107)

D. Joseph: A Literate Illiterate

The greatest challenge I had to face was how to translate Joseph's speech. My first attempt was to insert grammatical errors and Italian orthographic deviations. The result, however, read as if I had trivialized Joseph's character, and it appeared that the reader would be far more struck by the way I made him talk than by what he was saying. An example follows:

> No, it ain't, is about colours. You been saying is a novel 'bout the fall of man, but is really 'bout a dream. (Dabydeen 2005, 72)
>
> *No, non lo e. E' sui colori. Tu ai detto che e un racconto sulla caduta* **delluomo** *ma è veramente sul* **sognio**.
>
> *No, non lo è. E' sui colori. Tu hai detto che è un racconto sulla* **caduta dell'uomo ma veramente è sul sogno**.

The first Italian version contains the orthographic deviations and grammatical errors; the second is the same sentence without those errors. Both were disastrous in so far as they failed to replicate Dabydeen's specific use of language for this character. Joseph's role in the novel and the implications he carries with him are so important that I could not run the risk of devaluing him. In my final attempt I lowered the register, used colloquial forms; and where I was unable to find the right way to translate his language, I preferred to think as if he were speaking in Standard English, concentrating on the *matter* more than on the *form*. Returning to the above example, it becomes (with the colloquial form in bold italics):

> *No* **che** *non lo è, è sui colori. Tu* **stai qui a dire** *che è un racconto sulla caduta dell'uomo, ma* **veramente parla** *del sogno.*

4

My final concern was about the translation of the title. As previously stated, "the intended" is the fiancée of Kurtz in Conrad's *Heart of Darkness*. In the Italian published translation of *Heart of Darkness*, the intended character has been translated as "*la promessa sposa*", whose literal meaning is identical to the original version. However, when choosing translation strategies for Dabydeen's title *The Intended*, the translator has to consider a number of related issues. The first is whether *The Intended* makes the average British reader think of the character in Conrad's novel. I asked this question in an English forum and none of those who answered – all native speakers and well educated – made any reference to the female character of *Heart of Darkness*, but they all stated that "the intended" is an old-fashioned way to say "the fiancée". In the Italian translation, "*La promessa sposa*" has the same old-fashioned meaning, so I decided to propose it as the title. This title is also consistent with what Dabydeen's narrator actually says to Janet: "you are everything I intended" (Dabydeen 2005, 171), because in Italian we have the verb "*ripromettere*", which has the same meaning as "to intend", and the Italian version of the sentence "*tu sei tutto ciò che mi ero ripromesso*" can echo the title "*La promessa sposa*". Everything seemed quite straightforward; however "*La promessa sposa*" tends to remind the Italian reader of Alessandro Manzoni's *I promessi sposi*, one of the most important novels of Italian literature, which is read by Italian students in secondary school, and which has been adapted several times for Italian television. Again I spoke to friends and colleagues, this time asking the question: "if I say '*la promessa sposa*' what do you think about?" Everyone, from my cousin who left school at sixteen to my friend who is a teacher, replied "Manzoni" or "*I promessi sposi*". Conrad's novella neither came, nor will *ever* come into their minds. I therefore had to try a different approach, and switched the word order as to change the title to: "*La sposa promessa*". In this case, those who answered my question said neither Manzoni nor "*I promessi sposi*", nor, however, Conrad.

Translation is always a matter of choices. I believe that *The Intended* should be published in Italian with the title "*La promessa sposa*". Of course, the Italian reader will think of Manzoni's *I promessi sposi*, but this could also be beneficial in attracting the attention of the more inquisitive reader, who wonders what connection there can be between Manzoni and Dabydeen. Furthermore, anyone who buys "*La promessa sposa*" and is impressed or intrigued during the reading by Joseph's disquisition on *Heart of Darkness* may decide to read or re-read Conrad's novella, and will find in it the very same "*la promessa sposa*", therefore squaring the circle.

Notes

1. These are: rationalization; clarification; expansion; ennoblement and popularization; qualitative impoverishment; quantitative impoverishment; the destruction of rhythms; the destruction of underlying networks of signification; the destruction of linguistic patterning; the destruction of vernacular networks or their exoticization; the destruction of expressions and idioms; the effacement of the superimposition of languages.
2. The simple present of the Italian *andare* would be: *Io vado, tu vai, lui va, noi andiamo, voi andate, loro vanno*.

References

Ashcroft, B. 2001. *On Post-Colonial Futures: Transformations of Colonial Culture*. New York: Continuum.

Bandele, B. 1991. *The Sympathetic Undertaker and Other Dreams*. Oxford: Heinemann Educational.

———. 2007. *Nudo al Mercato*. Trans. B. Del Mercato; ed. P. Deandrea. Siena: Gorée.

Bassnett, S., and H. Trivedi, eds. 1999. *Post-Colonial Translation: Theory and Practice*. London: Routledge.

Berman, A. 1985. "Translation and the Trial of the Foreign". In *The Translation Studies Reader*, ed. L. Venuti, 276–89. London: Routledge.

Blake, W. 2009. "The Tyger". In *Canti dell'innocenza e dell'esperienza*. Milan: Feltrinelli.

Conrad, J. 1995. *Heart of Darkness*. London: Penguin (originally published 1901).

Dabydeen, D. 1990. "On Not Being Milton: Nigger Talk in England Today". In *The State of the Language*, ed. C. Ricks and L. Michaels, 3–14. Berkeley: University of California Press.

———. 2005. *The Intended*. Leeds: Peepal Tree Press.

Deandrea, P. 2006. "Dark Paradises: David Dabydeen's and Abdulrazak Gurnah's Post-colonial Re-writings of *Heart of Darkness*". Paper presented at "Rewriting/Reprising:

La reprise en literature" conference, University of Lyon: http://conferences.univ lyon2.fr/index.php/reprise/reprise/paper/view/42/78.
Deleuze, G., and F. Guattari. 1987. *A Thousand Plateaus: Capitalism and Schizophrenia*. Minneapolis: University of Minnesota Press.
Döring, T. 2002. *Caribbean English Passages: Intertextuality in a Postcolonial Tradition*. London: Routledge.
Ekwensi, C. 1961a. *Jagua Nana*. London: Hutchinson.
———. 1961b. *Jagua Nana*. Trans. G. Pignolo. Turin: Frassinelli.
———. 1993. *Jagua Nana*. Trans. P. Fattori. Rome: Edizioni Lavoro.
Farn, R. 2005. *Colonial and Postcolonial Rewritings of "Heart of Darkness": A Century of Dialogue with Joseph Conrad*. PhD dissertation, Faculty of Cultural Studies, University of Dortmund.
Fawcett, P. 1997. *Translation and Language*. Manchester: St Jerome Publishing.
Fee, M. 1993. "Resistance and Complicity in David Dabydeen's *The Intended*". *ARIEL: A Review of International English Literature* 24, no. 1: 107–26.
Gorra, M.E. 1997. *After Empire: Scott, Naipaul, Rushdie*. Chicago: Chicago University Press.
Granquist, R.J., ed. 2006. *Writing Back in/and Translation*. Frankfurt am Main: Peter Lang.
Lefevere, A. 1999. "Composing the Other". In *Post-Colonial Translation: Theory and Practice*, ed. S. Bassnett and H. Trivedi, 75–94. London: Routledge.
Maggioni, M.L., and P. Tornaghi. 2002. *Arcipelago Inglese. Diffusioni e futuro delle lingue inglesi nel mondo*. Milan: Sugarco.
Ramat Giacalone, A. 1973. "Italiano di stranieri". In *Introduzione all'italiano contemporaneo, la variazione e gli usi*, ed. A. Sobrero. Roma and Bari: Laterza.
Thieme, J. 2001. *Postcolonial Con-texts: Writing Back to the Canon*. London and New York: Continuum.
Tymoczko, M. 1999. "Post-Colonial Writing and Literary Translation". In *Post-Colonial Translation: Theory and Practice*, ed. S. Bassnett and H. Trivedi, 19–40. London: Routledge.
Venuti, L., ed. 2000. *The Translation Studies Reader*. London: Routledge.
Vermeer, H.J. 1989. "Skopos and Commission in Translation Action". In *The Translation Studies Reader*, ed. L. Venuti, 227–38. London: Routledge.
Vieira, E. Ribeiro Pires 1999. "Liberating Calibans: Readings of Antropofagia and Haroldo de Campos' poetics of Transcreation". In *Post-Colonial Translation: Theory and Practice*, ed. S. Bassnett and H. Trivedi, 95–113. London: Routledge.
Wordsworth, W. 2003. *Ballate Liriche*. Milan: Mondadori.

CHAPTER 5

Intertextuality and the "Spatialization" of Reading
Conradian Journeys in Dabydeen's *Disappearance*

RUSSELL WEST-PAVLOV

DAVID DABYDEEN'S WORK IS FREQUENTLY read against its intertextual precursors: Naipaul, Harris and Conrad. Such readings often bring out the emulatory or satirical stance of the author, thus reading for the contrastive effect of a writing that so overtly flouts its intertextual fabric. *The Intended* (1992) unmistakably gestures towards *Heart of Darkness* (Conrad 1990 [1899/1901]), but has also been explicitly identified by Dabydeen himself as a fictionalized biography of V.S. Naipaul and his attempt to remove himself from the Caribbean and leave behind Trinidadian life (Dabydeen 1993, 7). Jack and Fenwick in *Disappearance* (Dabydeen 1999) echo Naipaul's *The Enigma of Arrival* (2002) and Wilson Harris's *The Secret Ladder* (1963) (as suggested by the novel's epigraphs [Dabydeen 1999, vii]); Vidia in *The Counting House* (1997a) carries the same first name as Naipaul; and *A Harlot's Progress* (2000) clearly owes a debt to Hogarth. Another form of allusion may even be present in the Mrs Rutherford of *Disappearance*, referring obliquely perhaps to Anna Rutherford, the expatriate Australian academic at Aarhus who founded the Dangaroo Press, where Dabydeen published his first book of poetry (1984) and his first scholarly monograph (1987) (see Collet 1997, 25); or in the novel's references to Margaret Thatcher and her discourse of "Victorian . . . values" (Dabydeen 1999, vii, 153).

But all these identifications of intertextual links neglect what, following Foucault (1977/1994), one might call the "genealogy" of intertextuality: the non-originary process by which intertextual links are created in the process of writing and subsequently re-created in the process of reading. It is this double genealogy of intertextual production in writing and reading that the present chapter investigates in the context of a novel by Dabydeen whose title, *Disappearance*, itself refers to one of the moments in that process.

Intertextual Isomorphism?

The chapter seeks to lay bare a dynamic that precedes the effects generated by intertextual readings; namely, their very condition of possibility: that of a *spatially* configured montage- or palimpsest-like relationship of covering-exposure. The protagonist of *Disappearance* wonders whether Mrs Rutherford was "thinking of [her ex-husband] Jack but masking her emotions by an appearance of patriotism". He then extrapolates from that reflection on the lines of *pars pro toto*, asking himself "Whether the English fondness for recollections of past wars was not in fact a way of marking domestic crises which, overcome with the passage of years, had become mellowed and mildewed in the imagination" (Dabydeen 1999, 69). In the dialectic of "masking" and "marking", and the shift from the micro to the macro scales of memory, the force of traumatic events is attenuated, and the once-hidden can be re-integrated into public memorial narrative. In a curious inversion, it is perhaps the disappearance of the original force of the event that allows its marked trace to appear in public. Intertextual referentiality, one may conjecture, operates according to a similar dialectic, in which meaning emerges out of the gap left by erasure.

By tempting the informed reader to look for intertextual allusions and simultaneously frustrating that search, Dabydeen seeks to provoke a reflection upon the mode of functioning of intertextuality. To this end, he constructs, in *Disappearance*, a shadowy but finally elusive set of parallels with Conrad's *Heart of Darkness*, perhaps the key text of self-reflexive postcoloniality *avant la lettre* in twentieth-century writing. Similar to Mr Kurtz in *Heart of Darkness*, Mr Curtis in *Disappearance* is initially present only by hearsay, "appear[ing] on the scene" (Dabydeen 1999, 138) shortly before the end of the novel, as he crusades for the defence of the village against the encroaching sea. Like Kurtz, he is an "orator" and like Kurtz "he could have been the leader of an extreme party" (p. 149). ("Kurtz's proper sphere ought to have been politics 'on the popular side'... 'He would have been a splendid leader of an extreme party'" (Conrad 1990, 244).

Yet, despite such hints, the parallel between *Disappearance* and *Heart of Darkness* is remarkably unproductive, resisting further extension – or, rather, there are too many parallels running at cross-purposes. Is Mr Curtis to Mrs Rutherford as Kurtz is to the Intended? After all, Mrs Rutherford's first name is Janet (Dabydeen 1999, 95), and like her namesake in *The Intended* she provides the protagonist with clean clothes (pp. 3–4). Yet it is her husband Jack who apparently engages, during the couple's time in Africa, in Kurtz-like orgies, "abandoning [Mrs Rutherford] for native flesh" (p. 68), and is described as "mostly mouth and genitalia" (p. 141), recalling Kurtz "opening his mouth voraciously, as if to devour all the earth with all its mankind" (Conrad 1990, 224). Or is Mrs Rutherford, with "the knowledge of horror she possessed and was determined to proclaim", assailed by "a blinding illumination" (Dabydeen 1999, 103, 155; compare Conrad 1990, 239), herself a Kurtz figure who successfully returns to Europe, unlike the Conradian forbear?

There is therefore very little in Dabydeen's "phenotext" (to take Kristeva's [1972/1974, 83–86/1984, 86–90] early terminology) which is susceptible of a one-to-one mapping back upon Conrad's "genotext": "You sound like Curtis ... You are not Curtis", warns Mrs Rutherford significantly (p. 158). Indeed, Dabydeen may not be overly interested in such a one-to-one isomorphism, let alone in a real engagement with *Heart of Darkness* in the manner of the earlier novel *The Intended*. In an interview with Kwame Dawes, he has commented: "I suppose, when I look back at it, what I'm trying to do is to say that whereas our writers had to re-write the 'masterscripts' of Europe, my interest now, from another generation, is to re-write or respond to our ancestral writers ... Brathwaite, Selvon, Harris. ... so my particular interest now is fuck the 'master-scripts' [*sic*], let me write instead to Harris or Naipaul, write back, quarrel with, borrow from, love, praise, worship them" (Dabydeen 1997b, 210).

Conrad's *Heart of Darkness* is indisputably just such a "master-script" of European colonization, albeit one with a distinctly ambivalent stance with regard to that project. It is possible that Dabydeen's teasing refusal to allow the reader to construct a coherent set of relationships between *Disappearance* and Conrad's novella is evidence of his lack of interest in engaging primarily with the "master-scripts".

The single exception to the difficulty of positioning *Disappearance* unequivocally in relationship to *Heart of Darkness* appears to lie in the quasi-archetypal motif of the vitiated quest narrative culminating in a return (almost) to the point of departure. This motif can be located less at the level of individual characterization than at the larger structural levels of plot construction and indeed epistemological principles. In what follows I engage with this central motif and the manner in which Dabydeen adheres to or deviates from Conrad's template. It will become clear that his approach tends more towards the latter strategy, and that the crux of his postcolonial aesthetic in *Disappearance* resides precisely in that deviation.

The Round-Journey Motif

The protagonist's life trajectory (roughly summarized according to what Rimmon-Kenan [1983, 14–15] has termed "story-paraphrase") evinces a round-trip from Guyana to Britain and (almost) back again; the actual events related (the "discourse") begin in England then return to Guyana, before concluding in Britain (I am using the terms "story" and "discourse" as originally coined by Chatman 1978). Dabydeen constructs a chiastic interlacing of the round-journey motif with "story" and "discourse" structures as inverted mirror-images of each other: Guyana-Britain-Guyana ("story") and Britain-Guyana-Britain ("discourse") respectively. This chiastic interweaving concretizes the similarly chiastic concepts of journey-narrative ("story") and narrative-journey ("discourse"). By virtue of this double articulation of journey and narrative, Dabydeen can point towards the notion of a "spatialization" of meaning which is the very condition of possibility of reading – and of cross-cultural interaction. This motif can be understood as a meta-narratological topos referring to its own process of meaning-construction. Ultimately, nothing happens in this novel, so that it becomes an instance of what Todorov (1987, 53–54) has called a gnoseological or epistemological narrative: a narrative which emphasizes less the question: What will happen next? than the question: How do perceptions change in the course of the story? It is the utter absence of events which direct the reader's attention to the meta-narrative events of the book – and to the multidirectional writerly and readerly vectors of interpretation or reconstruction which constitute meaning.

The notion of a "spatialization" of meaning attains further significant resonances in the light of core meta-narratological *semes* such as Marlow's preference for tales whose "meaning . . . was not *inside* like a kernel but *outside*" (Conrad 1990, 138) or Mrs Rutherford's desire that "one day somebody like you would come *from far away* and disturb [the village idyll]. Like the *reverse of an English fairy tale*" (Dabydeen 1999, 158; emphases added). It is the journey-narrative (or the narrative-journey) which allows one to bracket these two topoi together. By narrating a journey from one place to another, or by journeying from one spatial instantiation of narrative to another, meaning is generated within an interstitial space. The meaning of a story, for Marlow, emerges out of its narration for an audience; the meaning of a national culture, for Mrs Rutherford, can only arise out of the journeys of English travellers when they leave home: "It made me know for the first time what we really are, *outside* of England" (p. 77; emphasis added). Meaning is not encapsulated within a narrative artefact or a national culture, but beyond it, and to fail to appreciate this is to fail to understand (national) narration. As a minor character in Rushdie's *The Satanic Verses* remarks, "The trouble with the Engenglish is that their hiss hiss history happened overseas, so they dodo don't know what it means" (1998, 343).

The journey allows a space of meaning-from-outside to be instantiated within the narrative. This notion emerges progressively in *Disappearance*, beginning with the simultaneous arousal and frustration of desire for knowledge by the archetypal quest-motif which underlies the topos of the journey and its vitiation. The narrative constantly frustrates the impulse to discover meaning within, "to find out the true nature of England" (Dabydeen 1999, 80), "to seek out England's story and make the connection you want" (p. 76) – in the finest tradition of Conrad, for whom "the inner truth is hidden" (1990, 183). Dabydeen's protagonist, drawn by "England in all its mystery" (Dabydeen 1999, 99), finds that "all that was left of England [is] a faint sense of mystery, enough to twitch your nose; a damp and musty smell . . . a palsied decay" (p. 133); "I'm beginning to think that nothing exists in England" (p. 157). Significantly, the narrator's host is equally energetically embarked upon a search for a hidden mystery, that of an essential otherness: "You're an African in spirit after all . . . you're an African deep down" (p. 104). The narrator disputes this "deep identity" (Bhabha 1987): "the many hours of probing into my psyche had suddenly yielded a secret she had planted there in the first place" (Dabydeen 1999, 104). What this double refusal of inward meaning suggests is not that there is indeed an essence of Englishness (in "the characterless and invisible English people of the village", p. 130) or of Africanness ("I knew nothing about Africa . . . I was no African", p. 7) but, rather, that essence is attributed within a process of reciprocal mirroring. The very act of probing constructs the probed interiority it then discovers. It is only when this process does not yield the expected results that other sites of meaning-making are laid bare.

At times, this process of an attributive search for meaning is almost consciously self-deconstructing. The protagonist sets up Mr Curtis as the heart of Englishness that he has sworn to sound out:

> I would make it my concern to engineer a meeting with Mr Curtis, I decided. Just as I wanted to build a dam for myself, so I wanted to establish him as a solid presence in my sight. The sparing and oblique references to him by Mrs Rutherford, and Christie's latest babbling, led me to believe that he held the key to the truth of Jack's disappearance. The mystery of Jack would at least give me *something* to engage with until my time came to return to Guyana. (p. 133)

Not unlike Conrad's Marlow, who spends a great deal of time waiting for rivets (Conrad 1990 [1899/1901], 173–78), so too Dabydeen's engineer experiences his English sojourn as that of a temporal hiatus needing to be filled by a task. Curtis is totally elusive, however, so that his disappearance merely anticipates the narrator's own disappearance. If the space of "return" initially seems to close an interval in which lack will be supplemented, the round-trip around which the novel is structured is in fact one which proceeds from lack to lack and back again – significantly, the protagonist leaves the village in a state of "empty-handedness" (Dabydeen 1999, 180). The journey's hollow trajectory is mirrored at the micro-level of the sentence: "The sparing and oblique references to him by Mrs Rutherford, and Christie's latest babbling, led me to believe that he held the key to the truth of Jack's disappearance" (p. 133): the phrasing progresses from the sceptical "sparing and oblique references" via a brief optimism in "led me to believe" and "the key to the truth" to a final collapse back into "disappearance". The sentence dramatizes exactly "writing as the disappearance of natural presence" ("*écriture comme disparition de la presence naturelle*"), as formulated by Derrida (1998, 159/1967, 228) in one of the epigraphs at the opening of the novel (Dabydeen 1999, vii). The sentence's own chain of alternating markers of absence and presence enacts the process of "making" and "masking" evoked at the outset of this chapter. The sentence emblematizes the very anticlimax of knowledge, culminating in the narrator's own "disappearance" – his literal "return to Guyana". This "disappearance" also adorns the cover of the novel, thus summarizing its project of vitiated knowledge as a whole.

"Disappearance" also possesses other textual implications. If the novel's "story-paraphrase" is about a round journey, what we are actually shown in the text's "discourse", however, is a single vector from Guyana to England. For, significantly, the return to Guyana is not described, but merely anticipated in part 3. Interestingly, this movement sketches the same vector as that of the post-war influx of erstwhile colonial subjects into Britain, a movement predicated upon the demise of the Empire and the colonial economy. As Naipaul's protagonist says in *The Enigma of Arrival*, "Fifty years ago there would have been no room for me on the estate" (Naipaul 1987, 55). Curiously, however, Dabydeen's text presents this post-war history a-chronologically, presenting the present before the past: "But what now that the cliffs around Hastings were collapsing as the Empire had crumbled?" (Dabydeen 1999, 121). This phrasing also performs a parallel spatial inversion. Rather than mimicking in its syntactic sequence the post-war influx from erstwhile colonial peripheries towards the putative mother country England, Dabydeen's phrase enacts a movement outwards from the metropolitan centre towards an erstwhile periphery ("cliffs" → "Empire"). The sentence's causal "story" is about a process of imperial erosion or "crumbling" which becomes more and more acute, and is manifested in increasingly concrete forms, as it attains the centre of the erstwhile Empire. What is performed as "narrative discourse", however, reverses this directional thrust, zooming outwards from the local geo-topological symptom ("the cliffs around Hastings were collapsing") to the broader world-historical cause ("the Empire had crumbled").

The "crumbling" of stable meaning and knowledge that is the true subject of the novel – and its frustratingly elusive *sujet* (or "discourse") in Shklovsky's (1990, 170/1929, 204) or Chatman's (1978) sense – thus takes place within a simultaneous two-way movement. The countervailing vectors of periphery-to-centre ("story") and centre-to-periphery ("discourse") co-inhabit the respective narrative levels of a single sentence. That sentence in turn is a synecdoche for the entire text whose epistemological problematic it crystallizes. The novel enacts, in its composite narrative strand, the two vectors of a round journey in which, by virtue of the similarly chiastic narrative-of-journey and journey-as-narrative, meaning "takes place", albeit in the very moment of its disappearance or dislocation.

The motif of the round journey thus contains a number of important principles of postcolonial narrativity and its concomitant epistemological implications. First, the round journey enacts an epistemological process which does not entail a return to an original meaning that is confirmed by being revisited. This circular journey does not offer the perspective of a closed circuit in which meaning is confirmed. Rather, the journey constitutes a sort of epistemological *via negativa*, in which true knowledge consists of realizing the inadequacy of knowledge. The two-way journey is thus susceptible, at first glance, of a merely negative definition: "There seemed to be no way into the village and no way out" (Dabydeen 1999, 91).

Yet, second, the crucial topos of learning, development and intellectual maturation is dependent upon this differential space. This circular peregrination transforms the traveller, thus bringing her or him back to a point of origin which is then perceived differently: the circular path stakes out a space of difference within which meaning can emerge. Meaning is a function of contrast, not of similarity. Far from bringing the traveller "back to the familiarity of the English sound of my voice, back to myself as an English person" (pp. 100–101), the journey renders the self alien to itself, and the familiar homeland foreign: "There's more wilderness here than Jack knew" (p. 97). This process of knowledge via spatial difference stands under the sign of axiological necessity: "there's no going back once you've started out" (p. 96). It is the "starting *out*", with its marker of exteriority, which guarantees true knowledge.

Finally, in accordance with the novel's constant overlaying of counter-directional vectors, the contrary actorial roles of the colonizers seeing themselves from abroad and the colonized arriving in Britain to scrutinize the English at home, are superimposed in the postcolonial moment of the "new commonwealth" influx. Previously, Mrs Rutherford's pedagogical task in Africa had consisted of giving her village pupils "a sense of our country being every bit as dark and diseased as we told them theirs was" (p. 71), and, in apparent contradiction to this precept, of persuading them "that England was not a place so foreign that they could not get there" (p. 71). This seeming paradox results in a contemporary synthesis of topo-epistemological alienation and self-knowledge: "the best histories of England are being written by black scholars" (p. 103). This perception-from-outside is the role attributed by the text to the protagonist: "For years those masks have kept me going because they're so odd, so different. They're like nothing I am, or any of us in the village. But after all this time I was getting used to them. Then you came along" (p. 13).

Knowledge arises out of an interstitial space, between us and them, I and you, here and there, coming and going. This space is imagined by Mrs Rutherford according to the exotic template of the initiation ritual: "For the first time in your life you disappeared from your tribe, held in isolation whilst undergoing all manner of trials and absorbing obscure wisdom held only by select elders. Afterwards you were returned to the tribe. You went back a stranger" (p. 11). Knowledge crystallizes in the ternary narrative sequence of /disappearance/ → /inculcation of wisdom/ → /return as a stranger/; the isolation of the initiate constitutes the interstitial realm where differential knowledge becomes possible. But there are less exotic instantiations of this search for meaning in the moment of departure from home and selfhood: "for a few seconds she retreated inwardly, trying to understand some truth about him, before returning to my company" (p. 13).

Mind the Gap!

Does Dabydeen's return to the company of the Conradian pre-text so as to construct his own work itself constitute such a round journey? Yes and no. In part, the incomplete journeys enacted within *Disappearance* are also replicated, in a sort of mega-synecdoche, at the level of Dabydeen's intertextual undertaking. This means, however, that the very motif of the round journey is subject to some brutal wrenching in Dabydeen's recycling, in accordance with a non-congruent notion of interstitial meaning-generation.

Conrad's narrative of the round-journey actually does culminate in Marlow's return, disappointing and tainted with mendacity as it may be. Marlow's circular journey is held in place, as it were, by the frame narrative. That bracketing narrative relativizes the discourse it contains by virtue of setting it within inverted commas (see Authier 1981) – those which mark Marlow's tale as a discourse-within-a-discourse. Yet it also endows it with a form of closure-from-outside by presenting it as a discursive object, a tale, despite its "inconclusive" (Conrad 1990, 141) and fragmented character. Dabydeen's novel has nothing of this structural neatness. *Disappearance* falls, rather, into three parts of uneven length, with some rather untidy overlaps. The three chapters in part 1 each begin in England and then revert rapidly to Guyana (Dabydeen 1999, 14, 23 and 38, respectively). In part 2, the predominantly English setting is disrupted once by a resurgent flashback to Guyana (the sections about Professor Fenwick and Annette, Dabydeen 1999, 81–91). In part 3, the return itself is anticipated but not described, subject to the same principle of instability as everything else in the text: "the slightest movement could cause it to flake and disappear" (Dabydeen 1999, 180).

Thus, by replicating but simultaneously dislocating the topos of narrative journey, Dabydeen amplifies rather than mutes the discrepancy between epistemological quest and fulfilment already staged by Conrad (the coast was "mute with an air of whispering, Come and find out"; but "The bush around said nothing, and would not let us look very far" – (Conrad 1990, 150, 188). At the level of intertextual productivity, Dabydeen deviates even further from Conrad's already existing deviation from the quest-motif (for example, Virgil, Dante, see Bowers 2006).

Intertextuality itself takes a prior "genotext" so as to construct a subsequent "phenotext", but then demands that the reader re-construct this process; the reader must work back from the "genotext" to the "phenotext" embedded within the texts held in her or his hand. But this return to the embedded "genotext" is never a pristine uncovering of an original meaning; it is far more a creative invention of a new meaning in the present of the reader. The "masking" of the intertextual meanings encoded in the body of the text demand a constant active process of "making" on the part of the reader which is predicated upon an un-"masking" whose outcome can never be predicted. Its prehistory, moreover, is that of a parallel but prior "making" on the part of the author which is then laid down in the text. The author's and the reader's "making" are not fundamentally different in nature – especially when the reader may her- or himself be an author in some other guise. The double intertextual process thus mimics the two-way journey and its attendant rogue proliferations of meaning.

Dabydeen reflects upon this process by imagining the present-day reader as a sort of time-traveller. The narrator, looking at the antique books in Mrs

Rutherford's sitting room, feels "intrusive and uncomfortable when I read them because I was from the future they could not envisage, a future which could well have brought terrors and disappointments to their evolving lives . . . I held the book guiltily and excitedly, as though I were a peeping Tom spinning fantasies from the partially glimpsed fragments of Albert's and Annie's lives, creating their past and future" (Dabydeen 1999, 9–10). This image of the reversibility of temporal vectors when a reader engages with a text is corroborated by Dabydeen's own comments on his artistic creation: "In none of my works is time linear, time is always doubled, the future determines the past, the future can affect the past. In other words, the way I behave, if I am part of the future of my people, revises other people's notion of who they were, you see: the future can impact on the past; and of course, the past always impacts on the present and the future" (Dabydeen 1993, 4). Reading is an anachronistic process taking us back to a past which, strictly speaking, can no longer be altered, but which none the less can be re-envisaged, re-imagined in the moment of reading.

The spatio-temporal paradox ("I was *from* the future") is important because it permits a two-way journey that is impossible within the dimension of temporality. Accordingly, in *Disappearance*, the two-way process of anachronistic reading is explicitly couched in spatial terms: "It was as if, instead of having to read the book page by page, I could . . . look through the tunnels made by the termites which bored through the whole text, and beyond, through the board covers, even into the substance of the desk or shelf that held the book, always making space, clearing space" (Dabydeen 1999, 10). But the condition of this anachronistic journeying, of this textual tunnelling, is the relinquishment of a comfortably stable, singular meaning. Like back-translation, intertextuality is a round trip which results in a dispersal of meaning rather than its gathering up in a moment of re-assembly.

Hermeneutic Circles

The motif of the round journey cannot but suggest one pre-eminent modern model of understanding, that of the "hermeneutic circle". In its exposition by the German philosopher Hans-Georg Gadamer (1965/2004), the "hermeneutic circle" is a conceit for the way the enquiring human subject's prejudices can be seen not as limitations to be overcome, but as the constitutive site in which any knowledge is anchored. The "hermeneutic circle" is a patently spatial metaphor for the process of understanding. At first glance, Gadamer appears to be concerned predominantly with the problematic nature of elucidating past traditions despite the temporal distance which separates us from them. But, significantly, he takes his notion of the circle from Heidegger (Gadamer 2004, 269/1965, 251). You have to jump into the circle, says Heidegger ([1927] 1984, 315/1962, 363), perhaps playing on the notion of the forest-clearing as an absence in which Being can become visible, thus paving the way for Gadamer's idea of prejudice as the non-understanding which is the necessary site for communication with an Other. It is the failure to do this which Mrs Rutherford reproaches her engineer guest in his endeavour to reconstruct the elusive Englishness he searches for: "you've been piecing bit by bit, objectively and mechanically, instead of letting your imagination rip" (Dabydeen 1999, 159). Imagination, dogged as it is by all the risks and limitations of subjective knowledge, nonetheless possesses the scope, despite its contingency, to allow meaning to emerge. Mrs Rutherford enjoins the protagonist to abandon his quest for objective knowledge and to accept the limitations (and powers) of subjectivity as the only possible site of knowing: "You were to have total freedom to make up the story of England, to interpret it with the same abandonment with which we described . . . your lot" (p. 159).

For Gadamer, prejudice or non-understanding can constitute a hermeneutic starting-point precisely because it will necessarily be challenged in the process of interpretation. The experience of interpretative reading is an experience in which the text poses a question to the reader (Gadamer 2004, 362/1965, 351). Dabydeen neatly encapsulates this recursive interrogation of the enquiring reader when he has his narrator say of Mrs Rutherford, "She put the question to me with such force that I sensed that she was addressing herself" (Dabydeen 1999, 157). "Address", of course, is a communicational mode with a directional inflection, because an "address" itself is a site on a topological grid. It is unsurprising, then, that Gadamer too imagines the process by which the interpreter's initial misunderstanding is questioned by the text in spatial terms: "the sense of the question is the only direction from which the answer can be given if it is to be right" (Gadamer 2004, 356, translation modified) ["*Der Sinn dessen, was richtig ist, muß von der einer Frage gebahnte Richtung entsprechen*" (Gadamer 1965, 346)]. In other words, the question points us in a direction (*Richtung*), sets us on a path, and that direction paves the way to right (*richtig*) understanding. Interpretation is a journey towards understanding. That journey is guided by questions, and the questions are posed by the other, the foreign.

The metaphor of the hermeneutic circle does not only describe the space into which we must step to begin the process of understanding. It also refers to a journey of understanding, one which starts out from our own prejudices, proceeding via an encounter with otherness – literary interpretation is an "experience of the other" (Gadamer 2004, 340) ["*Erfahrung des Anderen*" (Gadamer 1965, 329)] – and finally returns one to oneself:

> The life of the mind consists of learning to recognize itself in other being. The mind directed towards self-knowledge regards itself as alienated from the positive and must learn to reconcile itself with it, by recognizing it as its own and as its home. (Gadamer 2004, 341; translation modified)
>
> *Das Leben des Geistes besteht . . . darin, im Andersein sich selbst zu erkennen. Der auf sein Selbsterkenntnis gerichtete Geist sieht sich mit dem "Positiven" als dem Fremden entzweit und muß lernen, sich mit ihm zu versöhnen, in dem er als das Eigene und Heimatliche erkennt.* (Gadamer 1965, 329)

Gadamer sees the inevitable contingency of our mortal human knowledge as a limitation that Enlightenment epistemology has rejected, turning it into an otherness within the knowing self. Only by accepting that otherness within can we know the other, he claims, finally returning to home to true self-knowledge in the process.

However, whereas Gadamer posits a process of increasing understanding through the engagement with the Other (text, epoch and culture), Dabydeen, appropriating Conrad and amplifying the latter's already powerful scepticism, emphasizes the Derridean "openness" of "writing and meaning", evoked in one of the novel's four epigraphs (Dabydeen 1999, vii). It is the interval between instances of meaning and the deferral of closure which, though frustrating the desire for meaning, makes the space of interpretation possible in the first place.

It is tempting to concur with the rather sour verdict of a critic such as McWatt (1997, 121), who concludes that "Dabydeen's point [is] that there is little substance at the centre of the self-consciously post-colonial text – no story apart from the enactment of theoretical paradigms." Yet if *Disappearance* never ties up its loose narrative ends, never brings its protagonist back to his point of departure in the satisfying closure of the return journey, this is not merely an illustration of the way the postmodern-postcolonial text is constantly "disappearing... up its own aporia" (p. 122). Dabydeen is suggesting, rather, that the accumulating history of colonialism and postcolonialism is the very ground upon which cultural meanings, willy-nilly, have been generated over the past centuries. This territory (diasporic, exilic, nomadic, and made up of journeys which never culminate in an exact return to the point of departure, of a "rhythm of depositing and shifting" [Dabydeen 1999, 177]) is the condition of possibility of cultural renewal and artistic creativity: "You were to have total freedom to make up the story of England" (Dabydeen 1999, 159).

References

Authier, J. 1981. "Paroles tenues à distance". In *Matérialités discursives*, ed. B. Conein et al, 127–42. Villeneuve d'Ascq: Presses Universitaires de Lille.
Bhabha, H.K. 1987. "Interrrogating Identity". In *Identity: The Real Me*, 5–11. ICA Documents 6. London: Institute for Contemporary Art.
Bowers, T. 2006. "Conrad's Aeneid: *Heart of Darkness* and the Classical Epic". *Conradania* 38, no. 2: 115–42.
Chatman, S. 1978. *Story and Discourse: Narrative Structure in Fiction and Film*. Ithaca: Cornell University Press.
Collet, A. 1997. "An Interview with Anna Rutherford". In *Teaching Post-Colonialism and Post-Colonial Literatures*, ed. A. Collet, L. Jensen, and A. Rutherford, 22–29. Aarhus: Aarhus University Press.
Conrad, J. 1990. *Heart of Darkness*. In *Heart of Darkness and Other Tales*. Oxford: Oxford University Press (originally published 1901).
Dabydeen, D. 1984. *Slave Song*. Sydney: Dangaroo Press.
———. 1987. *Hogarth's Blacks: Images of Blacks in Eighteenth Century Art*. Manchester: Manchester University Press.
———. 1992. *The Intended*. London: Vintage.
———. 1993. "Making Creative Use of Cultural Tensions: An Interview with David Dabydeen". *Hard Times* 49: 4–11.
———. 1997a. *The Counting House*. London: Vintage.
———. 1997b. "Interview with Kwame Dawes". In *The Art of David Dabydeen*, ed. Kevin Grant, 199–221. Leeds: Peepal Tree Press.

———. 1999. *Disappearance*. London: Vintage.
———. 2000. *A Harlot's Progress*. London: Vintage.
Derrida, J. 1967. *De la grammatologie*. Paris: Minuit.
———. 1998. *Of Grammatology*, trans. G. Chakravorty Spivak. New ed. Baltimore: Johns Hopkins University Press.
Foucault, M. 1977. "Nietzsche, Genealogy, History". In *Language, Counter-Memory, Practice: Selected Essays and Interviews*, ed. D. Bouchard, 139–64. Ithaca: Cornell University Press.
———. 1994. "Nietzsche, la généalogie, l'histoire". In *Dits et écrits, 1954–1988*, ed. D. Defert and F. Ewald, vol. 2, 136–56. Paris: Gallimard.
Gadamer, H. 1965. *Wahrheit und Methode: Grundzüge einer philosophischen Hermeneutik*. 2nd ed. Tübingen: J.C.B. Mohr/Paul Siebeck.
———. 2004. *Truth and Method*, trans. J. Weinsheimer and D.G. Marshall. Rev. ed. London: Continuum.
Harris, W. 1963. *The Secret Ladder*. London: Faber.
Heidegger, M. 1962. *Being and Time*, trans. J. Macquarie and E. Robinson. New York: Harper and Row.
———. 1984. *Sein und Zeit*. 15th ed. Tübingen: Max Niemeyer (originally published 1927).
Kristeva, J. 1972. "Quelques problèmes de sémiotique littéraire à propos d'un texte de Mallarmé: Un coup de dés". In *Essais de sémiotique poétique*, ed. A.J. Greimas, 208–34. Paris: Larousse.
———. 1974. *La Révolution du langage poétique: L'avant-garde à la fin du XIXe siècle: Lautréamont et Mallarmé*. Paris: Seuil.
———. 1984. *Revolution in Poetic Language*, trans. M. Waller. New York: Columbia University Press.
McWatt, M. 1997. "'Self-Consciously Post-Colonial': The Art of David Dabydeen". In *The Art of David Dabydeen*, ed. K. Grant, 111–22. Leeds: Peepal Tree Press.
Naipaul, V.S. 1987. *The Enigma of Arrival*. London: Picador.
Rimmon-Kenan, S. 1983. *Narrative Fiction: Contemporary Poetics*. London: Methuen.
Rushdie, S. 1998. *The Satanic Verses*. London: Vintage.
Shklovsky, V. 1929. *O Teorii Prozy*. Moscow: Isdatelstovo Federacija.
———. 1990. *Theory of Prose*, trans. B. Sher. Elmswood Park, IL: Dalkey Archive Press.
Todorov, T. 1987. "Les deux principes du récit". In *La Notion de littérature et autres essais*, 47–65. Paris: Seuil/Points.

CHAPTER 6

David Dabydeen's *A Harlot's Progress*
Re-presenting the Slave Narrative Genre

ABIGAIL WARD

DAVID DABYDEEN'S NOVEL *A Harlot's Progress* (1999) takes its title from a series of prints from 1732 by William Hogarth. Each picture is a scene in the ironic "progress" or, rather, decline of the harlot, beginning with her arrival in London and culminating in her death from venereal disease. Dabydeen accentuates his book's relationship to these images by providing details or fragments of the prints at the start of each of the nine sections of his book. Though this is a novel less directly preoccupied with art and artists than his long poem *Turner* (1994), he remains both fascinated and worried by the production and continued reception of representations of black people into the twentieth century.[1] As Mungo, the eighteenth-century protagonist of *A Harlot's Progress*, predicts, "centuries from now, when your descendants think of a Negro, they will think of a pimp, pickpocket, purveyor of filth" (Dabydeen 2000, 273).

In Hogarth's series, the black servant appears in just one of the six plates, but is bestowed a narrative centrality by Dabydeen. *A Harlot's Progress* is the tale of Mungo (also named Noah and Perseus), an African captured into slavery by the notorious Thomas Thistlewood, at the hands of whom he suffers both physical and sexual abuse, and brought to Britain. He is prepared for sale by a washerwoman named Betty, and sold at a coffee shop auction to Lord Montague. Following Lady Montague's illness and her husband's subsequent uneasiness at having him in the house, Mungo runs away to assist a Jewish quack doctor, Mr Gideon, and ends his days "treating" – in reality, poisoning – diseased prostitutes. There, he meets the dying Moll Hackabout, the central character of Hogarth's study. The text, mainly narrated by Mungo, begins some thirty years after the publication of Hogarth's prints. Now an old man, Mungo is reluctantly speaking his tale to Mr Pringle from the Abolition Society in return for basic necessities.

Slave narratives were instrumental to the abolitionist movement, and it would seem there was an increasing relevance of the stories of these early "black Britons" to late-twentieth-century Britain, where slave narratives played an important role in claims of black people's legitimacy of habitation in the United Kingdom. As James Walvin argued in *An African's Life: The Life and Times of Olaudah Equiano, 1745–1797* (1998): "Equiano is more popular today than ever before. Pictures of Equiano festoon any number of dust-jackets, his face is used on posters to promote exhibitions and TV programmes. He has his own postcard issued by an English museum . . . It is worth reminding ourselves that, a mere thirty years ago, very few people knew who Equiano was. In the course of a generation, he has gone from anonymity to international fame: a best seller in Africa, North America and Britain" (Walvin 1998, 194).[2]

Walvin's book was published exactly thirty years after Enoch Powell's "Rivers of Blood" speech; Equiano's burgeoning relevance in the thirty years following this moment may be seen to arise from a need to understand the historical precedence for black habitation in Britain in order to counter racist claims of the newness of the country's black presence.[3] This need to understand the history of the black presence in the United Kingdom runs alongside an increasingly widespread identification in both Britain and North America with Equiano's articulation of the complexities of a diasporan identity.

While it would seem there is a growing, and important, movement towards remembering the early black British presence, Dabydeen suggests – in his concerns about the reception of slave narratives – that such figures need to be remembered sensitively. The experiences of his narrator bear witness to the exploitation ingrained in the slave narrative genre, whether at the hands of the abolitionist editor or the voyeuristic reader. Dabydeen suggests in *A Harlot's Progress* that interest in these texts may be in part due to a morbid fascination or voyeuristic titillation at reading stories of bondage and cruelty exercised against black people.

Although Dabydeen has called *A Harlot's Progress* "a novel by Equiano . . . A novel about arriving at the state of writing. In the way that Equiano had to in the eighteenth century" (Stein 1999, 29), this is not a canonical engagement with the eighteenth century.[4] In narrating Mungo's story, Dabydeen chooses not to ventriloquize the voices of Sancho or Equiano – figures already heavily overrepresented – but rather writes the story of an unvoiced black presence. Mungo, at the same time, is a stereotyped figure; as Jack Gratus has noted, "the black man as a figure of fun . . . Had names by which he could easily be identified and placed like Sambo and Mungo" (Gratus 1973, 178). Dabydeen's comment that Equiano "had to" write in a particular manner is especially pertinent; as I shall show, Dabydeen suggests through his character Mungo the ways in which slave narrators have, in "speaking" their stories, also been spoken for. There are constant reminders of what Mungo's readers will or will not tolerate, and he has economic reasons for his adherence to matters of audience – as he informs his fellow slave, Ellar, "they can refuse to buy my book, and I'll starve" (Dabydeen 2000, 256).

Mungo is uneasy with his British readership, all too aware of the constrictive form of the slave narrative and fearful of "alienating his readers" (p. 256). In his continued critical reappraisal of the slave narrative genre, Dabydeen also proposes that the authors of narratives may not be who they purport to be – we see the heavy-handed role of abolitionists, as "editors", in shaping the narrative: "the book Mr Pringle intends to write will be Mungo's portrait in the first person narrative. A book purporting to be a record of the Negro's own words (understandably corrected in terms of grammar, the erasure of indelicate or infelicitous expressions, and so forth)" (p. 3). The use of "portrait" reinforces the connection to art and visual representation, as befits a novel based on a series of pictures. In indicating the artistry behind Pringle's representation of Mungo, this quotation also suggests a certain way of looking at his slave narrator. Pringle's role in the narrative is, therefore, that of an artist, "resolv[ing] to colour and people a landscape out of his own imagination" (p. 3). As I have already indicated, this is a process not devoid of voyeurism or exploitation.

Pringle's proposed role in shaping Mungo's tale serves as a reminder that it is unwise to assume that slave narratives were actually representative of slaves – the slaves "writing" their tales were inevitably anglicized, and often had much assistance in constructing their stories. In depicting the methods by which Mungo is prevented from fully narrating his own story – bound by conventions of form and readership – Dabydeen reveals the problematic nature of the slave narrative genre; his figure is silenced even as he attempts to represent himself. One might make a comparison between Mungo's struggle for self-representation and the ways in which Equiano and Sancho in particular have been represented – for example, as figureheads for black Britain. While there may be a tendency to view slave narrators as representative of black people in the eighteenth century, as Walvin has suggested, he has also been clear to point out that Equiano and Sancho "were not *typical* of other blacks in London; both were well known, had caught the imagination, and both were literate" (Walvin 1998, 160). Although both men have come to be seen as representative of the eighteenth-century black presence in London, it is important to remember that their very literacy, which brought them fame, also differentiated them from other black people in Britain at this time. By exposing the constructed and performative nature of identity and the anglicized manner of slave narrators, Dabydeen questions the degree of authority invested in them as spokespersons for black Britain.

While exploring the complex relationship between editor and slave narrator, Dabydeen goes as far as comparing Pringle to the slave captain John Newton. In so doing, he interrogates the virtue of abolitionists, implying that the move from slavery to abolition is a process of "conversion" that can work either way: "Perhaps I should not make such a trial of his Christian soul and convert him to the ways of slavery. I watch his fingers bunch into a secret fist, as if he would cuff me for my rebelliousness . . . The pen is in [his hand] as if waiting to sign a warrant for my arrest, or my sale" (Dabydeen 2000, 7). Pringle is, it would seem, as capable of being a slave owner as an abolitionist, the pen able to sign Mungo's sale as much as write his tale – or, indeed, it would seem that in writing his tale, Pringle is also "selling" Mungo: "[Pringle] draws his breath nervously like a virgin waiting to be laid bare and rested on white sheets. He takes up pen with unsteady hand, but has to blot a drop of ink that drips involuntarily from the nib . . . He pants across the page as I dictate" (p. 177). Pringle's dripping pen(is) suggests his voyeuristic excitement at hearing Mungo's tale; his sexual exploitation of the slave narrator leads Mungo to conclude: "he makes me feel like a strumpet whose performance is undeserving of his coin" (p. 178). Mungo's literal and metaphoric "whoring", alongside his centrality in the novel, intimates he is the "harlot" of the novel's title. In comparing Thistlewood's literal whoring of Mungo to Pringle's metaphorical prostitution of him, Dabydeen proposes there may be reason to worry about the enslaving and exploiting nature of the slave narrative genre and the indulgence of pornography lurking within such tales. It should perhaps come as no surprise, therefore, that Mungo also feels exploited by Hogarth's portrayal: "once I was affordable only to the very rich, a slave worth countless guineas, but because of Mr Hogarth I was possessed, in penny image, by several thousands" (p. 274). Mungo is thus whored by Hogarth, as well as by Pringle, indicating that eighteenth-century representations of black people in Britain may well have been fatally compromised by their form. As I shall illustrate shortly, it could be argued that the "consumption" of these black figures has not ceased with the end of the slave trade.

In addition to Pringle's heavy-handed control of the narrative, much of Mungo's tale is also fabricated, indicating a continuing resistance to narrating his story: "memory don't bother me, that's why I don't tell Mr Pringle anything. I can change memory" (p. 2). "Truth" is unavailable in this text – what matters is the way in which the past is invented, manipulated and bought – for, as Lord Montague comes to realize, "truth itself was hostage to the designs of stockjobbers, another commodity changing hands at a price" (p. 199).

Mungo's rebellion against the form of the slave narrative encompasses his refusal to demonize Thistlewood or create the kind of representation Pringle wants to hear about: "Mr Pringle's version of Captain Thomas Thistlewood is untroubled. Captain Thistlewood is a demon and I his catamite" (p. 75). As Elizabeth Kowaleski Wallace has argued, in this novel Thistlewood is marginally more than just a "pederast taking masochistic pleasure from the body of a boy slave"; he is provided with "a complex, if perverted, psychology. In particular, Thistlewood reverently worships a mythical lost Albion" (Kowaleski Wallace 2000, 245). He is, indeed, especially sensitive to the changes in England, largely ushered in by the flourishing slave trade – he tells Mungo to "forget the land" (Dabydeen 2000, 69), meaning Africa, but strives to take his own advice.[5] England in the mid-eighteenth century is not the homeland he wishes to remember. In Thistlewood's nostalgia for a lost England we find the idea of a deliberately forgetful past and a refusal to take responsibility for the slave trade that has altered and shaped England beyond recognition.

To Thistlewood, slaves are ultimately animals, and the slave ship is therefore a deathly ark: "he tended to them not as soulful beings but as sick animals ... He was deeply affected by the loss of his creatures" (p. 50). Mungo ironically compares this to Hogarth's prints of animals being mistreated: "You,

English, inhabitants of a country distinguished for its adoration of pets and charity to the lesser breed, will know the tempest of emotions that overcame my Captain. You have the nightmare of Mr Hogarth's genius, in his series of prints, *Scenes of Cruelty*, to stir you to patriotic rage" (p. 50).

Again, like his questioning in his poem *Turner* of the motivation behind J.M.W. Turner's representation of the jettison of live slaves in 1781 from the slave ship *Zong*, Dabydeen questions why Hogarth would want to paint – and people would want to own – these images: "the fatal beating of a horse, the tormented dog, the blinding of a dove – that you have purchased . . . in their thousands to adorn your mantelpiece and conscience" (p. 50). While Hogarth apparently created these pictures "with the hope of in some degree correcting that barbarous treatment of animals, the very sight of which renders the streets of our Metropolis so distressing to every feeling mind" (Antal 1962, 10), Dabydeen suggests a more sinister reason for their acquisition. It is intimated in *A Harlot's Progress* that Hogarth's audience takes a sadistic pleasure from looking at images of cruelty, and also from being chastised for their transgressions – by extension, the motivations of the reader of slave narratives are also brought into question. Mungo notes that, "to ensure that his book sells, he will not repel his readers by calling them necrophiles" (Dabydeen 2000, 257), articulating the notion that there is something voyeuristic and underhand about the readers' expectations of what lies within the narratives.[6]

Writing of his collection of poems *Slave Song* (1984), Dabydeen claimed that "the British Empire . . . was as much a pornographic as an economic project" (Dabydeen 1989, 121) and, while Dabydeen's Thistlewood amply demonstrates the "pornographic" reaches of Empire, he is not the only white Briton in *A Harlot's Progress* to harbour sadistic views towards Mungo. As if to clinch the suggestion of the potentially improper reception of these texts, Dabydeen includes in his novel a depiction of the voyeuristic reader in the character of Lady Montague. When Mungo strikes another servant in front of Lady Montague, his action has a profound effect: "There was no denying the pleasure – an inexact word, but she could think of no better – in following the news of the massacre, like the sharks (so it was sensationally reported) scenting blood and swarming to the tragic spot. Her imagination, so bounded by her surroundings, found sudden release in the descriptions of sharks feasting on men's flesh; men bound and chained, unable to resist or to retaliate with the violence glimpsed in [Mungo's] violent utterance, violent act" (Dabydeen 2000, 222).

Restricted by her position as a wealthy woman in eighteenth-century Britain, Lady Montague yearns for the sadomasochistic violence she reads in the sensational descriptions of the *Zong* massacre printed in the newspaper reports. This can be aligned with what Kobena Mercer has referred to in *Welcome to the Jungle* (1994) as the "certain ways in which white people 'look' at black people and how in this way of looking, black male sexuality is perceived as something different, excessive, Other" (Mercer 1994, 173).[7] The means by which Lady Montague achieves a temporary "release" is, therefore, in perusing descriptions of bondage and violence specifically directed towards black people. However, this will remain a short-lived freedom; the sadism will be once more restricted, or "bound", in being edited from Pringle's narrative. As Mungo complains: "*He don't want no dirt of woman but Moll's kind so I cannot tell more of Lady Montague's madness ... To him, a Lady is not ever improper, and if she is, it can never be in print. Life and print: two different things*" (Dabydeen 2000, 225–26; italics in original). In contrast, Mungo is all too aware of what Pringle *does* want to hear about – "he wishes me to tell him that I was ripped from my mother's breast by the evil slaver Captain Thistlewood, taken to his ship and so molested that I became a willing disciple to the ways of animals" (p. 70). Like Lady Montague, Pringle also craves the sensational or pornographic, pandering to his abolitionist readers' desire to hear of "evil" slavers and innocent slaves.

Mungo soon realizes that, ultimately, if he is to survive, he must overcome the guilt of both having survived thus far, and of having done so by submitting to exploitation. *A Harlot's Progress* therefore explores the necessity of learning to survive guilt; Mungo tells Betty "stories suckled from Captain Thistlewood, of Sparrowhawk and Owl, of Thistle and Cowslip and Pennyroyal, their ancient fame and magical properties which survive the guilt that makes men murder men, and build their shining governments of the damned" (p. 150). The end of this passage paraphrases the Guyanese poet Martin Carter's words in his poem "After One Year": "Men murder men, as men must murder men, / to build their shining governments of the damned" (Carter 1999, 108). In the same year that Dabydeen published *A Harlot's Progress* he also edited a new edition of Carter's *Selected Poems*. These poems were largely written to signal Carter's discontent with the colonial government of mid-twentieth-century Guyana; in Gemma Robinson's words, Carter "was among a dissatisfied generation of colonial people who would resist the life that had been mapped out for them by the British Empire" (Carter 1999, 17). Despite the apparent differences in subject matter between the two works, connections can be traced, culminating in this paraphrasing of the last two lines of Carter's poem within the text of Dabydeen's novel. This draws *A Harlot's Progress* not only firmly into the twentieth century, but also into a connection with Guyanese politics and the struggle for freedom, suggesting a wider application of notions of enslavement and liberation.[8] Men, of course, were quite literally murdering men in the course of slavery – the case of the *Zong* being a particularly brutal example. The money from the trade was benefiting not only the merchants but also the government, enabling the construction of Britain's eighteenth-century "shining governments of the damned". Also, Carter's poems are, as Robinson notes, first and foremost about resistance. So, too, I have argued that in *A Harlot's Progress* we see Mungo's repeated resistance to the life and genre "mapped out for [him] by the British Empire", in his refusal to conform to Pringle's desired narrative and to his white readers' pornographic demands – indicating that resistance is an essential component in the continuing survival and struggles of black people in both Britain and her former colonies.

The link to Carter's work is not, however, the only twentieth-century connection in the novel. Dabydeen has commented that, although *A Harlot's Progress* depicts "England from eighteenth century black eyes [*sic*]", it also "has resonances of today; it's eighteenth century only in form" (Stein 1999, 29). Published just over fifty years after the arrival of the *Empire Windrush*, Dabydeen's novel dwells in the eighteenth century, but also points to a more recent mid-twentieth-century British past. One of these resonances includes Thistlewood's forgetful England, which can be aligned with the historical forgetfulness of those white Britons who view the *Windrush* as the first black British arrival. However, arguably the most important resonance for Dabydeen concerns the ongoing reception of representations of black people within Britain.

While Dabydeen's novel serves as a necessary reminder of the eighteenth-century black presence in London, it also illuminates the problems of slave narratives. It cautions us that such works have to be taken in context as products of the abolitionist movement and that the slaves "writing" these tales were severely restricted by issues of form, readership and editors. Additionally, *A Harlot's Progress* reveals the perversion behind such tales and the danger of a pornographic response to their publication. Dabydeen's book therefore imaginatively adds the motivation and thoughts behind the slave narrative – the irritation at issues of editing, register and tone, for example, all suggest the complexity of his slave narrator. Mungo's frustration at the limits or checks forced upon him by the genre also indicate the ways in which slave narrators have simultaneously been "spoken for" in narrating their stories, as Sancho lamented, "from Othello to Sancho the big – we are either foolish – or mulish – all – all without a single exception" (Sancho 1968, 218).

In the genre of the slave narrative, the "pornography of Empire" (Dabydeen 1989, 121) had found a form that simultaneously bound the narrator while flagellating the reader; writing at a time when slavery was still legal, slave narrators found that these chains had yet to be loosened. Black people were exploited by more than just slavery in the eighteenth century – slave narrators were appropriated for different causes; used to advertise products and promote public houses, overtly constructed and overrepresented. However, the twentieth-century casting of slave narrators as icons may be seen as another form of enslavement, in stripping these early black Britons of their complicated humanity. While recognizing the continuing importance of these figures to twentieth-century Britain, Dabydeen suggests in *A Harlot's Progress* that it is imperative to acknowledge their complexities in order to begin lightening the burden of representation.

Acknowledgements

A version of this chapter was previously published as "David Dabydeen's *A Harlot's Progress*: Re-presenting the Slave Narrative Genre", *Journal of Postcolonial Writing* 43, no. 1 (2007): 32–44.

Notes

1. For more on Dabydeen's poem *Turner* and the provocative comparison between the artist J.M.W. Turner and a slave-ship captain, see Ward (2007).
2. The irony here is that this image is no longer thought to be a portrait of Equiano; see, for example, King 1997, 35–36.
3. Other books exploring the early black British presence include Peter Fryer's *Staying Power* (1984), in which Fryer reminds us that black people have lived in the United Kingdom since Roman times, and Ron Ramdin's *Reimaging Britain* (1999).

4. There are elements of other slave authors in Dabydeen's creation of Mungo; Ignatius Sancho, for example, was a butler to the Duke and Duchess of Montagu.
5. As "Britain" was a relatively new concept created by the Act of Union of 1707, the land Thistlewood yearns for is a nostalgic England.
6. Ironically, Dabydeen's critique of the reader of works about slavery has implications for his own audience. In *The Postcolonial Exotic*, Graham Huggan discusses what he calls "ethnic autobiographies"; such postcolonial texts, he suggests, "signal the possibility of indirect access to 'exotic' cultures whose differences are acknowledged and celebrated even as they are rendered amenable to a mainstream reading public" (Huggan 2001, 155). Dabydeen's novel may also be read as an ironic comment on this kind of writing. It would seem that it is not simply visual art that has the potential to exploit black people; as Dabydeen implies in *A Harlot's Progress*, written texts may also fuel readers' perceived desires for "exotic" stories about slavery.
7. Mercer's particular focus here is on the work of Robert Mapplethorpe – most notably *Black Males*. As Mercer notes, "it is as if, according to Mapplethorpe's line of sight: Black + Male = Erotic/Aesthetic Object . . . The 'essence' of black male identity lies in the domain of sexuality" (Mercer 1994, 173).
8. Another connection is, of course, Britain's establishment of the colony of British Guiana in 1831.

References

Antal, F. 1962. *Hogarth and His Place in European Art*. London: Routledge and Kegan Paul.
Carter, M. 1999. *Selected Poems*, ed. D. Dabydeen. Leeds: Peepal Tree Press.
Dabydeen, D. 1989. "On Not Being Milton: Nigger Talk in England Today". In *Tibisiri: Caribbean Writers and Critics,* ed. M. Butcher, 121–35. Sydney: Dangaroo Press.
———. 2000. *A Harlot's Progress*. London: Vintage.
Fryer, P. 1984. *Staying Power: The History of Black People in Britain*. London and Sterling: Pluto Press.
Gratus, J. 1973. *The Great White Lie: Slavery, Emancipation and Changing Racial Attitudes*. London: Hutchinson.
Huggan, G. 2001. *The Postcolonial Exotic*. London and New York: Routledge.
King, R. 1997. "Ignatius Sancho and Portraits of the Black Élite". In *Ignatius Sancho: An African Man of Letters,* ed. R. King, S. Sandhu, J. Walvin, and J. Girdham, 15–43. London: National Portrait Gallery.
Kowaleski Wallace, E. 2000. "Telling Untold Stories: Philippa Gregory's *A Respectable Trade* and David Dabydeen's *A Harlot's Progress*". *Novel* 33, no. 2: 235–52.

Mercer, K. 1994. *Welcome to the Jungle: New Positions in Black Cultural Studies*. New York and London: Routledge.

Ramdin, R. 1999. *Reimaging Britain: Five Hundred Years of Black and Asian History*. London and Sterling: Pluto Press.

Sancho, I. 1968. *Letters of the Late Ignatius Sancho: An African*, ed. P. Edwards. London: Dawsons of Pall Mall.

Stein, M. 1999. "David Dabydeen Talks to Mark Stein". *Wasafiri* 29: 27–29.

Walvin, J. 1998. *An African's Life: The Life and Times of Olaudah Equiano, 1745–1797*. London and New York: Continuum.

Ward, A. 2007. "'Words Are All I Have Left of My Eyes': Blinded by the Past in J.M.W. Turner's *Slavers Throwing Overboard the Dead and Dying* and David Dabydeen's *Turner*". *Journal of Commonwealth Literature* 42, no. 1: 47–58.

CHAPTER 7

"To Say Profitably"
Dabydeen's Exoticist Aesthetic

ERIK FALK

1

IN ONE OF DAVID DABYDEEN'S early poems – the title poem of *Coolie Odyssey* – the poet reflects on the difficulties of being a Caribbean poet voicing the past in a late modern metropolitan setting. "Now that peasantry is in vogue" the poem begins, "Poetry bubbles from peat bogs" and other rural locations (Dabydeen 1988, 13). For the Caribbean poet, this gives an "occasion for speaking", to use George Lamming's phrase, but it also gives him a sense of exploiting his history and his family. While poetic expression recalls the realities of village life – the grandmother, unchanging as the "canefield and whiplash"; or the villagers "Roopram the Idiot", Harilall, Chandra, Poonai – its public function is serving up tales of misery and woe to an audience hungry for exotic reality (pp. 9–10).[1] Through the poem, the speaker also questions his own motives. Recall involves a risk of getting things wrong: the grandmother he portrays protests (possibly ventriloquized by the poet's own voice) against being put in a poem – "*Is foolishness fill your head. / Me dead. / Dog-bone and dry-well / Got no story to tell*" – and the ancestors, who have gone mute "like texts", do not disclose much either (p. 12; italics original).

The poet, in other words, is engaged in a deciphering that has its pitfalls. Yet he "persists" in his need for stories. More seriously, the poet admits that remembrance entails a double act whose other side is the profitable exploitation of cultural difference:

> Still we persist before the grave
> Seeking fables.
> We plunder for the maps of El Dorado
> To make bountiful our minds in an England
> Starved of gold
>
> (p. 12)

The dilemma remains unsolved and the poem ends with the bitter comment that the role of the Caribbean poet is to deliver stories of West Indian "folk" misery to an audience of middle-class metropolitans:

> We mark your memory in songs
> Fleshed in the emptiness of folk,
> Poems that scrape bowl and bone
> In English basements far from home,
> Or confess the lusts of beasts
> In rare conceits
> To congregations of the educated
> Sipping wine, attentive between courses –
> See the applause fluttering from their white hands
> Like so many messy table napkins
>
> (p. 13)

The theme of the poem – the dilemma that (communal) self-expression unfolds through adaptation to a demand for stereotypes – is nothing new. Indeed, it was one of the tenets of Lamming's 1960 diagnosis of the cultural and experiential world of the exiled Caribbean author that he or she had to conform to the writing patterns of "Dickens, Jane Austen, Kipling and that sacred gang" (2004, 27). What gives the theme a different bend in Dabydeen's poem is the emphasis on the economics of the situation, and the implication that there is something to be *gained* for the poet who lives up to the expectations. The poet speaks, but he acknowledges that as he does so he capitalizes on memories and does in fact receive the reward of the applauding audience.

The theme is emblematic of Dabydeen's writing, and scenes like the ones in "Coolie Odyssey" appear throughout his literary work. Yet it has received little attention to date in the criticism on Dabydeen's poetry and fiction.[2] In what follows, I will engage some of the scholarship on the "postcolonial exotic" to situate the theme of connected economies of value, money and sentiment in Dabydeen's fiction, and analyse textual performance as it relates to this nexus. My argument will be twofold. First, I will claim that Dabydeen's literary production displays an exoticist aesthetic that wavers between submission to (felt) audience expectations of narratives of Caribbean misery, barbarism and "folk" culture (and occasionally magic) on the one hand, and a metathematic which comments on and undercuts the referential character of these descriptions on the other. Second, that this aesthetic is linked to a preoccupation with literary exoticism as a mode of sentimentalist thinking. This preoccupation is best exemplified through his latest fiction, where interwar working-class England is subjected to the same exoticizing strategies that were previously used on the Caribbean. The analysis of exoticism as what could be called a mature aesthetic, I will suggest, contributes to the ongoing mapping of the "postcolonial exotic" of recent fiction.

2

The notion of "postcolonial exotic" is directly connected to the increasing influence of writers and artists from so-called marginal cultures and regions that several critics have commented on.[3] In the last decade, the trend has been more systematically analysed through the term "postcolonial exotic" by Graham Huggan (2001), who made it central in his *The Postcolonial Exotic: Marketing the Margins* and Sarah Brouillette's *Postcolonial Writers in the Global Literary Marketplace* (2008) is largely a response to Huggan.[4] These studies, which are as sociological as they are literary, begin from two central premises: that postcolonial literature exists successfully in a literary *market* and caters to groups of readers who are also consumers, and that postcolonial literary studies has become a discipline successful enough to warrant scepticism towards some of the radical political claims that seem to be part of its self-understanding.

Huggan's founding assumption is that "cultural difference" has over the last few decades become a commodity which a globalized publishing industry sells to an audience demanding representations of this difference. A cadre of academics give these writers the mark of distinction by analysing their work alongside a rhetoric of radical politics. With the waning of the barrier between writers and critics, Huggan uses the phrase "writers/thinkers" as the professional group which gives the ideological alibi for the ongoing commodification, and thereby signals the merging of the producers and professional consumers of the literature in question. To account theoretically for this process he develops a distinction between *postcolonialism* and *postcoloniality*. Where the former is an "anti-colonial intellectualism that reads and valorizes the signs of social struggle in the faultlines of literary and cultural texts", the latter is a "value-regulating mechanism within the global late-capitalist system of commodity exchange" which bestows value on "culturally 'othered' goods" (Huggan 2001, 6). The two work in tandem; postcoloniality by valuing cultural difference, and postcolonialism by "certifying" the goods that are sold as culturally different, through a particular politically inflected jargon and through the authority of its practitioners.

For Huggan, the commodification of cultural difference has two consequences. It entails a reduction of real difference into an "almost sameness" that is still different enough to be exciting for a mainstream consumer (p. 22). But it also forces writers and thinkers into becoming uncomfortable representatives of their "original" cultures (even "original" cultures that are hybrid). On the one hand they sell cultural difference to a metropolitan audience and are seen as representing that difference; on the other, since they are more often than not émigrés, and commodification allows only for simplified and reduced versions of cultural difference, they will never be truthful in their depictions although they must appear so. They are unreliable informants pressed into serving an audience with the tales it demands, and they have repeatedly to "stage" their marginality in order to gain authority. In so doing, they become strategically "exoticist" rather than exotic: "these writers/thinkers are not only subject to, but also actively manipulate, exoticist codes of cultural representation in their work" (p. 20).

Sarah Brouillette both nuances and challenges Huggan's argument. She demonstrates that the concentration of ownership in publishing and media conglomerates has led to both streamlining and diversification (Brouillette 2008, 27). The literary market has been divided up into niches, and the "cultured circuit" of intellectually trained readers now constitutes one – even several – economically viable markets. This tendency parallels the acknowledgement of the buying power of various ethnic or cultural communities, which are consequently seen as profitable market segments in their own right (pp. 55–56). Postcolonial novels, in other words, are profitably marketed and sold to more or less academic audiences around the world. Rather than the "general" cosmopolitan reader Huggan postulates, she states that there are a number of readerships, many of which are more or less specialized in literary areas.

The investigation into the readerships of postcolonial literature has consequences for the idea of the "exotic" as well as for the political significance of the field itself. Brouillette adopts Huggan's controlling analogy between postcoloniality and tourism, but argues that the idea of "staging" is untenable since no clear distinction exists between the true and the "staged" (pp. 26–31). The division between readers is more rhetorical than actual; it sets up a distinction between two types of readers: the naïve, general, metropolitan reader who demands the exotic, and the sophisticated reader (like Huggan) who sees through the exotic to the strategic usage of its codes. The usefulness of the tourism analogy, she argues, lies not in the division into tourists and non-tourists, but in the desire of people in both areas to separate themselves out from the crowd (p. 25). Postcolonial critics and their slightly less specialized colleagues are not less touristy; instead they are engaged in a game of positioning within an academic field (p. 174).

3

The profitable exploitation of cultural difference lies at one end of a thematic polarity that recurs through Dabydeen's fiction. The other pole is cultural mimicry, or, more precisely, the resistance against being regarded as culturally different. In *The Intended*, for instance, the protagonist gradually erases his rural Guyanese origins as he strives for complete inclusion in English culture. The protagonist learns to speak what Benita Parry (1998, 1) has called "Cambridge English", learns to read Joseph Conrad's *Heart of Darkness* as a story of a timeless spiritual journey and not of imperialism, and is finally admitted into Cambridge. To make the point that his university entry coincides with the disappearance of the last traces of Caribbean identity, the story ends with him climbing into a taxi to be, symbolically as well as literally, "gone" (Dabydeen 2000, 246).

The poem *Turner*, an *ekphrasis* based on J.M.W. Turner's painting *Slavers Throwing Overboard the Dead and Dying – Typhoon Coming On*, focuses on cultural difference and effacement in terms of cultural memory. The poem's speaker (the slave in the foreground of Turner's painting) recalls memories of an idyllic childhood before "Turner" and his slaver gang arrive. These memories blend with later instances of exploitative language acquisition at the hands of "Turner" – who is now the captain of the ship that takes the slaves away – and the result is that the past is filtered through a language and cultural codes of empire. The "native schemes" to counter the invasion, for instance, look suspiciously like the Christian crucifixion – an event and a religion that, of course, arrives with the slavers: "Premeditations to spear his side, spill / The magic from his wrist, sacrifice / Him to a withered babla tree" (Dabydeen 2002, 29). The impact of subsequently learned language on the early memories also puts in doubt the veracity of the memories of village life, which is described as unchanging habit and idyll (p. 10). Entry into the English language and its cultural codes, the poem shows, is violent, and means that memories mutate and the past can no longer be accessed in its original state. But it also opens an always ambiguous possibility for gain; "Turner" teaches the captives to "say profitably / In his own language, *we desire you, we love / You, we forgive you*" (p. 40), and "profit" here refers as much to the use "Turner" may put the slaves to as what the slaves might earn from speaking forgiving words at the right time.

In *A Harlot's Progress*, this thematic reaches its most complex form. The novel recounts the story of Mungo, a freed slave, whose narrative of captivity is taken down by the abolitionist Pringle. Here, as in *The Intended*, the theme of cultural difference is cast in an imagery of visibility, and involves storytelling and profit. Mungo is aware that Pringle will use his story to champion his own case and thus make him "visible" – "And I, Mungo, am to prick the nation's conscience by a testimony of suffering, which Mr Pringle will compose with as much intelligence as a Jewish conspiracy. For I am to become a crucial instrument in Mr Pringle's scheme to rescue England from its enemies" (Dabydeen 1999, 144) – and so refuses to submit to the narrative script Pringle makes for him. But he is also a "ruined archive", in Pringle's phrase, whose memories of his origins have become unsettled by later cultural learning. The result is that he delivers a number of contradictory accounts – even as he admits that he succumbs to Pringle's scheme out of pity (p. 8). One example of the contradiction is the account of the mark on his brow. In a first account, it is punishment for his trespass into forbidden territory in his African village; in the second, it is a mark of evil; in the third version it is the branded initials of his master (pp. 19, 31, 75).

I have written elsewhere on the significance of the intricate narrative arrangement of *A Harlot's Progress*, and so will not repeat my reading in detail (Falk 2007, 130–45). Here it is enough to state that the competing voices – some of which are "impossible" breaches of the conventions of narrative level – make it impossible to extract from the reading an authoritative account of Mungo's experiences. This means in turn that Mungo remains, as it were, in the dark, unfettered by the constraints of representation. In contrast to the artist Hogarth, whose painting of the narrative's prostitutes, like Pringle's story, aims at evoking "nothing more worthy than pity in the viewer" (Dabydeen 1999, 272), Mungo's manifold and contradictory accounts avoid becoming the fixed narrative object of a sentimentalist aesthetic.

4

From the examples given above, it could be argued that Dabydeen's fiction critically investigates cultural difference. Through an imagery of visibility and themes of cultural memory and cultural effacement, it seems to put into question the possibility of reaching back into or recounting an authentic past. It represents memory as a fragile resource impressionable by linguistic and cultural codes, and shows the stereotypical exotic imagery the protagonists rely on. But there is a paradox here: the representations, even as they are negated or unsettled, are present and remain in the texts. Negation does not mean erasure. As Tobias Döring has observed with reference to *Turner*, the "negative in language cannot erase without also creating something to erase; in doing so it gives life to what it tries to kill" (1998, 201). What is thematized as flawed or erroneous – the result of the workings of British language and codes upon an impressionable mind – is positively still there in the text. Whereas the thematic of his fiction critically reflects on the exploitation of "folk", for instance, Dabydeen's texts circulate the same exotic imagery of cultural difference and could thus be accused of capitalizing on (memories of) "folk" culture by spicing them up for a metropolitan audience. If the "postcolonial exotic" entails reduction and decontextualization of representations of cultural difference, then, one must conclude that not only Dabydeen's protagonists but his actual texts engage in it.

The double commitment to a critical thematic of cultural stereotype and textual proliferation of stereotypical imagery is precisely what Huggan refers to as "strategic exoticism". Ultimately, for him, it is a melancholy strategy. As the ongoing commodification turns cultural difference into marketable goods, the only real alternative – recourse to a *true* representation of cultural difference untainted by market forces – has all but disappeared. What remains for the (sophisticated) reader is to chart the ways in which postcolonial literature registers the pressures of commodification through their staged marginalities. For Brouillette, too, strategic exoticism is melancholy, but her attention to aesthetics allows her to be more particular about *towards what end* strategic exoticism works. In her discussion on Derek Walcott, she contends that the end is "de-exoticization" – a conscious distancing from the people the writer is supposed to represent, and a refusal to serve as guide in literary clothing (Brouillette 2008, 27). This, as we shall see, is not Dabydeen's end.

5

One of the striking features of Dabydeen's fiction, which my remarks above have already signalled, is its intensely intertextual character. Two of his texts are directly related to artistic predecessors: *Turner* and *A Harlot's Progress*, but all his works are full of literary and cultural allusions (Falk 2007, 120–23). The "revisions" of Turner's and Hogarth's works are not merely indexes to a preoccupation with literary history as a form of cultural memory, as Döring has noted (2002, 147); it is also an exploration of the role of the artist under conditions of commodification of culture.

The use of Hogarth is not coincidental. Dabydeen belongs to Huggan's category of "writers/thinkers" and devoted part of his (early) academic career to historical studies of British culture in Hogarth's time. The result was two books on eighteenth-century British culture: *Hogarth's Blacks* (1985) and *Hogarth, Walpole and Commercial Britain* (1987). Central in both works is the claim that the rise in commercial activity connected to imperial expansion during the eighteenth century affected large groups in society and transformed, or at least threatened to transform, social relationships. In cultural debates and the public view there was, Dabydeen concludes, persistent anxiety that the commercialization of reality would dehumanize society and turn social relations into artifice. Chief examples of this emerging social artifice were "foreign" characters such as the prostitute (who was socially different) and the black (who was racially or culturally different). In the realm of art, the popular artist Hogarth, in Dabydeen's view, exemplifies this commercialization in his propensity to adapt to the current tastes of his patrons and "exploit" current topics in order to "make capital" out of popular sentiments (Dabydeen 1985, 17–40; 1987, 15–40). Dabydeen's analysis of Hogarth's series is shared by Mark Hallett, who has commented on the series' double voice, which was apparent even to contemporary viewers: the depiction of the harlot's "progress" (really her downfall) is simultaneously empathetic and pornographic and invites (male) spectators to mourn the exploitation of the innocent woman while it simultaneously offers a "fantasy of sexual invitation and availability" (Hallett 2000, 85). Hogarth, in this way, could align himself both with the moralists and the pornographers and was able to capitalize on the images of society's less fortunate and the desires of the art-consuming public.

In comparison to the openly declared double investments of *A Harlot's Progress*, Turner's 1840 painting appears morally unequivocal. Turner was a vehement abolitionist, and the painting was intended to show the horrors of the slave trade. Originally meant to be exhibited beside the brightly coloured *Rockets and Blue Lights (Close at Hand) to Warn Steam Boats of Shoal Water*, it was to contrast an immoral past with a technologically and morally superior present (Hamilton 2003, 47). But there is an ambiguity to Turner's painting (Fulford 2006). In the words of Ian Baucom, the ambiguity is part of a Romantic aesthetic that encourages sentimental meditation on the (horrible) past in order to stir empathy, but then tempers any feelings of outrage or injustice by signalling that the events belong to an era that is irrevocably gone (Baucom 2005, 274–80). Turner's painting, Baucom states, is an "experiment in interestedness" that itself "satisfies any demand for justice" by letting the spectator empathize with the suffering slaves and then mentally turn away from the "damaged past" (p. 281).

Dabydeen's scholarly and literary interest in artists like Hogarth and Turner amounts, unsurprisingly perhaps, to a reflection on his own artistic position. For, obvious differences aside, Hogarth, Turner and Dabydeen have something in common as artists. They all exploit social and cultural issues, transform them into aesthetic objects, and capitalize on "popular feeling". More precisely, they exploit figures of social or cultural difference for aesthetic – and possibly commercial – gain. If this is the case, the generalization to make from Dabydeen's artistic practice appears an addendum to Huggan's and Brouillette's mappings. Whereas they investigate the recent emergence of the "industry" of postcoloniality, Dabydeen's aesthetic suggests that this is the last phase of a centuries-old development of commercialization of culture that is intrinsic to capitalist modernity.

6

A closer look at Dabydeen's specific use of exoticism will substantiate the point made above. For even as the theme of invisibility could be taken to "de-exoticize" cultural difference – to the extent that unrepresentability (Mungo's multiple and contradictory stories) entails an escape from the reductive confines of representational literature or art – this strategy still relies on circulating the very exotic images that are negated. More importantly, however, the exotic in Dabydeen's fiction has arguably become more pronounced. In his latest novel (although the tendency is foreshadowed in his earlier works and relatively explicit in *Our Lady of Demerara*) this is visible in a shift from material to methodology: *Molly and the Muslim Stick* displays an exoticizing strategy that turns the ostensibly familiar into something strange and foreign.

In *Molly and the Muslim Stick* – which is part of the Macmillan Caribbean Series and thus marketed as a text representative of the region – the exotic blends with the fantastic. Related to Wilson Harris's literary universe of metamorphoses and merging of dream and reality, the novel signals its dedication both to the recognizably concrete and the strangely fairy-tale-like from its opening sentence: "Once upon a time – the night of Wednesday 26th October 1933, when I was fifteen – it happened" (Dabydeen 2008, 1).[5] The narrative moves through different Northern English locations to end in Demerara, where spiritual rebirth is both promised and denied. The novel's protagonist Molly, who has travelled there in search of her one-time Amerindian lodger, finds that the arrival of an earlier white missionary and his murder by the villagers has forever changed the place and drawn it into debased and violent modernity. The "shock of the new, death by a human act" amounts to the loss of primordial innocence (p. 167). Estranged from her English origins and disoriented in her Guyanese surroundings, Molly is left, like the beadless tribe in *Turner,* in cultural exile, and waits at the end of the novel for a tide to take her away somewhere she can reinvent herself (Dabydeen 2002, 36; 2008, 176).

The narrative contains a number of descriptions of cultural difference that oscillates between the destitute and the magical and between the sublimely unrepresentable and the stereotypical. Molly finds that Georgetown has "stupendous wooden architecture, the most graceful and natural buildings I have seen", but also that it has "no museums or galleries, nothing to attract a tourist", and that Demerara is "swamp or sanatorium" (2008, 149, 150, 157). Om's village and his culture, on the other hand, initially offer her a place and a time to reflect on her life: "I was going on, going on, going on. Rambling and scrambling. So after two weeks of doing nothing, going nowhere, just collecting and recollecting random items, trying to find some kind of pattern, what have I discovered?" (p. 154). Molly's Amerindian friend is a Demerara villager named "Om" by Molly and her Stick for "ethnic edge", and so in his name combines Hindu, Muslim and Christian-Orthodox connotations. At the same time, the "dominating" zero-like "O" of his name suggests that he cannot fully be captured in representation, as does his fantastic language, a combination of "Sanskrit and a Greek dialect", or "more like Aramaic than anything else" according to Molly's companion Stick (pp. 101, 92).

The theme of debasement and renewal that plays out geographically through a juxtaposition of England and Guyana clearly invests in and manipulates exotic imagery, and much could be said about the representation of the foreign in this novel – especially since it undercuts a straightforward association of value with place. But descriptions of the Caribbean are not the subject of my comments here. I want instead to focus on something initially much less exotic.

The novel begins with a detailed account of the miserable circumstances of Molly's upbringing. Already on the first page, the reader learns that she is sexually abused by her father, on the following page that she is also beaten, and a few pages later that she becomes an unwilling prostitute to her father's friends. The descriptions are matter-of-fact and distanced despite the first-person narration. This is how the first instance of abuse is described: "Dad came home, banging the front door to signal his drunkenness and frustration. I had covered my face with a blanket, but he peeled it back, exposing me to his want. I struggled when he lifted my night-shirt, but then I surrendered, imitating Mum in her quiescent state" (p. 1). Molly's abuse is representative of the debased culture of the town where she lives, and the misery of the present is put in sharp contrast to an idyllic past. Maureen, Molly's mother, at one point reads "a book" of local history or legend and tells her husband-to-be about a past golden age: "Accrington's nothing today, a piece of grime, but it wasn't always so you know" (p. 19). To his scepticism – "What else could it have been?" – she replies with a narrative of the region's history: "long before the pits and chimneys there was a forest. People lived in a little clearing, beside a stream. There were deer and trout. Women wove mats from reeds, made clay pots, clothes from the fur of animals, wine from wild berries . . . In the olden days Accrington was like the sound of gilded harps, not what blares out from Salvation Army brass" (pp. 19–20).

These descriptions do not belong to a realist aesthetic of any kind, and they are not intended to approximate accounts of experiential reality.[6] They are representations reduced to dramatic essentials, calculated to stir emotional responses, and they draw on the same rhetoric of sentimentality as the poet in "Coolie Odyssey", the anonymous narrator of *The Intended*, the slave in *Turner*, and Mungo in *A Harlot's Progress*. And they are, as in the earlier works, often explicitly designed by the various narrators to achieve a certain effect. Molly, for instance, subsequently feeds her lover's "curiosity for northern life" with her clichéd stories (p. 51).

There is, however, an important difference between this later novel and the earlier examples, where the profitable exploitation of cultural difference was coupled with a thematic of difficult remembrance due to the speaker's or narrator's culturally "marginal" position. In the current case, the representations are of that which should be relatively familiar to a Western metropolitan audience: working-class life in Accrington, Lancashire, between the World Wars. If one is allowed to generalize from these brief examples, the employment of the exotic in *Molly and the Muslim Stick* reveals that it has less to do with material than with approach. Exoticism results not because the *already foreign* (to a Western metropolitan audience) is filtered through narrow representational codes; it happens rather when the *relatively familiar* (to a Western metropolitan audience) is transformed into something foreign and strange.

7

The exoticizing textual strategy, I would like to suggest, continues into the present the sentimentality that inhabits exoticism. As Chris Bongie (1991) has demonstrated in his historical study of literary exoticism, the initial optimism of the discourse of exoticism is gradually replaced by a pessimism that addresses the loss of the exotic.[7] From the late eighteenth century, he notes, when exotic cultures existed simultaneously with but geographically apart from the modern world which encountered them, there is a growing conviction that modernity is actually eliminating the geographical and cultural "elsewhere". With modernity taking on global proportions, as it was seen to do already towards the end of the nineteenth century, the loss of the exotic appears total (Bongie 1991, 5).[8] The result of the aggressive spread of modernity is that the "elsewhere" which exoticism relies on mutates: from a *spatial* location that is far away but accessible, it becomes a *temporal* location that is irrevocably lost but can be lamented or aesthetically recalled. In their melancholy efforts to recall a past irretrievably gone, the Romantic aesthetic and the exoticist discourse sustain one another.

Dabydeen arguably writes in a late-modern era where the exotic has transformed yet again. It can no longer be recalled even temporarily in art, and so it returns as simulacrum – that is, as tourist spectacle. Both Huggan and Brouillette elaborate an analogy between the "postcolonial exotic" and tourism to stress the artifice of the images presented. But where Huggan decries the falsification this literary tourism entails, Brouillette argues that tourism and postcolonial literature both exist in a *post*-tourist phase, which is signified by a disbelief in the possibility of reaching authentic cultural experiences. Because it recognizes that authenticity is irrevocably gone, it is "a kind of elegiac performance" (Brouillette 2008, 41).

Elegy, however, is only one side of Dabydeen's aesthetics. The other side is what could be called, for lack of a better phrase, profitable immersion. Dabydeen's elaboration of an exoticist aesthetic amounts to a statement that even if distinct authentic cultural difference no longer exists, the *sentimentality* that was one of the driving forces in the exoticist "project" (as Bongie calls it) remains, and nourishes a demand for signs of cultural difference. This demand can be profitably exploited. If modernity in its late phase has obliterated *both* the possibility of encountering authentic cultural otherness *and* of artistically recalling an untainted version of the past in Romantic fashion, the exoticist stories must abandon their pretence at referential truth. The exotic, then, does not exist but can be *manufactured* and sold to satisfy the desire for sentiment, compassion and pity. From a historical discourse which purports to represent reality more or less truthfully, exoticism mutates in the hands of Dabydeen into a literary strategy which becomes almost purely performative; it creates the exotic it represents, and may, hypothetically at least, turn anything into an exotic commodity.

8

Huggan and Brouillette's analyses of the "postcolonial exotic" are much-needed investigations into the "industry of postcoloniality". They shed important critical light on some of the industry's self-images and their methods and data allow them to resituate postcolonial literature, and postcolonial authors, within a framework of ongoing commodification of cultural difference. Their commitment to extra-textual factors leaves questions to be answered, however, as to the precise strategies, goals and textual effects of exoticism and textual analysis still has something to offer here. This is the case not least with "writers/thinkers" like Dabydeen, who are highly attentive to the developments of which he himself and his fiction are an integral part. In this article, I have discussed Dabydeen's simultaneous involvement in and negotiation of the exotic imagery Huggan and Brouillette map, but I have also argued that his preoccupation with themes of commodification of narrativized cultural difference as well as the textual/inter-textual performance of his fiction illuminate aspects of the role of the author in a late-modern world of ongoing commodification. Dabydeen's analytical contribution, as it were, is to acknowledge the long and entwined historical roots of exoticism and discursive sentimentality which places the author – however unlikely this may seem from a point of view which celebrates the radical cultural politics of postcolonial fiction – at the tail end of a history that includes both Hogarth and Turner.

To Dabydeen, the imperially expanding Britain experienced (the threat of) an increasing commercialization of reality that accompanied the loss of (the idea of) authentic behaviour and culture. Hogarth's art registered this loss in its theatricality and the endlessly staged interpretive games; in Dabydeen's words, the challenge "to speculate and indulge in a hectic chase after meaning" that his paintings invite the viewer to participate in (Dabydeen 1985, 12). Turner's art responded to a different kind of loss – of particular (rural) landscapes, cultures, and peoples, and did so by aesthetically recalling, reflecting on and laying this past to rest. Dabydeen's exoticist aesthetic unfolds in a late-modern world that is "post" the idea of authentic cultural difference, even as memory. The exotic in this phase transforms into simulacrum: it can be produced in order to satisfy desires for the sentimental, but its images will make no pretence of referring to reality.

Notes

1. Exactly what images of "folk" the poet presents to his audience can, of course, never be established, since the doubling of poetic address and audience introduces a gap between what *they hear* and what *we read*.
2. My *Subject and History* (2007) contains an overview of Dabydeen scholarship.
3. Stuart Hall, for instance, commented on the "powerful space" of marginality in the early 1990s (quoted in Kalliney 2008, 16) and Robert Young a few years later saw marginality as part of a wider trend where opposition, subculture and radicalism in potentially all its forms were being transformed into sellable sign-objects (1996, 109).
4. Other critics have used the term along slightly different or similar lines. Susheila Nasta (2005, 294–343) means by "postcolonial exoticism" a reading which expects postcolonial novels to "write back" to a certain European literary canon and which therefore risks missing other cultural echoes. Chris Bongie (2003) and Peter Kalliney (2008) have made insightful contributions to the discussion of the exotic(ist) investments of postcolonial literary studies.
5. The similarity to Harris, which in turn continues a line of allusions to Harris and Walcott in *Our Lady of Demerara*, arguably represents a widening intertextual frame of reference, from a predominantly British cultural archive to include renowned Caribbean authors and works. It is outside the scope of this article, however, to discuss this in detail.
6. From a narratological point of view, it could be argued that representations like these may not be true (Maureen gets her information from a "book"), or may express the views of the narrator and character, respectively, and not of the text as a whole. Such distinctions have little relevance here. My point is that the text displays the *same* exoticism on *different* narrative levels and so subscribes to an overall exoticizing aesthetic.
7. For the relationship between sentimentality, exoticism and imperialism, see also Mary Louise Pratt's discussion of the explorer Mungo Park as sentimental adventurer (1992, 71–85 especially).

8. The historical exoticism that Bongie discusses aimed at recovering "the possibility of 'total experience'" – that is to say, complete experiential participation in society – that "traditional societies" allowed but which had ostensibly been lost in modern societies (1991, 9). Bongie's usage of the term thus appears contrary to Huggan's and Brouillette's, which describes a falsified or reduced representation of experience. The two overlap, however. Bongie notes that exoticism, apart from its truth-seeking version, also came in *imperialist* (seeking dominance over the foreign) and *exoticist* (privileging the foreign as superior) forms (p. 17). The distinction between them is, in practice, not easy to draw. Huggan and Brouillette, however, simply by virtue of the *relevance* of their analysis, imply that the value of the exotic is underpinned by a desire for cultural difference that may be a desire for authentic otherness, or for representations of an inferior or superior culture.

References

Baucom, I. 2001. "Globalit, Inc.; or, The Cultural Logic of Global Literary Studies". *PMLA* 116, no. 1: 158–72.

———. 2005. *Spectres of the Atlantic: Finance Capital, Slavery and the Philosophy of History*. Durham, NC: Duke University Press.

Bongie, C. 1991. *Exotic Memories: Literature, Colonialism and Fin de Siècle*. Stanford, CA: Stanford University Press.

———. 2003. "Exile on Main Stream: Valuing the Popularity of Postcolonial Literature". *Postmodern Culture* 14, no. 1: 1–54.

Brouillette, S. 2007. *Postcolonial Writers in the Global Literary Marketplace*. Basingstoke: Palgrave.

Dabydeen, D. 1985. *Hogarth's Blacks: Images of Blacks in Eighteenth Century English Art*. Manchester: Manchester University Press.

———. 1987. *Hogarth, Walpole and Commercial Britain*. London: Hansib.

———. 1988. *Coolie Odyssey*. London: Hansib and Dangaroo.

———. 1998. *The Intended*. London: Vintage.

———. 1999a. *A Harlot's Progress*. London: Jonathan Cape.

———. 1999b. *Disappearance*. London: Vintage.

———. 2002. *Turner: New and Selected Poems*. Leeds: Peepal Tree Press.

———. 2008. *Molly and the Muslim Stick*. Oxford: Macmillan Caribbean.

Döring, T. 1998. "Chains of Memory: English-Caribbean Cross-Currents in Marina Warner's *Indigo* and David Dabydeen's *Turner*". In *Across the Lines: Intertextuality and Transcultural Communication in the New Literatures in English*, ed. W. Kloss, 191–204. Amsterdam: Rodopi.

———. 2002. *Caribbean-English Passages: Intertextuality in a Postcolonial Tradition*. London: Routledge.

Falk, E. 2007. *Subject and History in Selected Works by Abdulrazak Gurnah, Yvonne Vera and David Dabydeen*. Karlstad: Karlstad University Press.

Fulford, S. 2005. "David Dabydeen and Turner's Sublime Aesthetics". *Anthurium* 3, no. 1: http://scholar.library.miami.edu.anthurium/volume_3/issue _1/fulford.

Gilroy, P. 1993. *Small Axe: Thoughts on the Politics of Black Cultures*. London: Serpent's Tail.

Hallett, M. 2000. *Hogarth*. London: Phaidon.

Hamilton, J. 2003. *Turner: The Late Seascapes*. New Haven: Yale University Press.

Huggan, G. 2001. *The Postcolonial Exotic: Marketing the Margins*. Routledge: London.

Kalliney, P. 2008. "East African Literature and the Politics of Global Reading". *Research in African Literatures* 39, no. 1: 1–23.

Lamming, G. 2004. *The Pleasures of Exile*. Ann Arbor: Michigan University Press.

Nasta, S. 2005. "Abdulrazak Gurnah, *Paradise*". In *The Popular and the Canonical: Debating Twentieth-Century Literature: 1940–2000*, ed. D. Johnson, 294–343. London: Routledge.

Parry, B. 1997. "Between Creole and Cambridge English". In *The Art of David Dabydeen*, ed. K. Grant, 47–66. Leeds: Peepal Tree Press.

Pratt, M.L. 1992. *Imperial Eyes: Travel Writing and Transculturation*. London: Routledge.

Young, R. 1996. *Torn Halves: Political Conflict in Literary and Cultural Theory*. Manchester: Manchester University Press.

CHAPTER 8

Re-scripting Genealogies
Or, On the Purpose of (Re)writing in David Dabydeen's *Our Lady of Demerara*

LILIANA SIKORSKA

IN DINAH CRAIK'S SHORT STORY "The Half-Caste", a young girl, Zilla, is described by the narrator as "a girl with an olive complexion, full Hindoo lips, and eyes very black and bright" (Craik 2000, 337). Until we discover that she is a rich heiress, she is patronized by those around her, even by her benevolent governess, the narrator, not because she is young and inexperienced but because her dark complexion makes her little more than a savage, wild and untamed, almost a child of nature, happy in her ignorance of civilization and unhappy with the education that is forced down her throat. At the end of the story, when Zilla marries her benefactor and has children of her own, the same narrator describes Zilla's daughter as a "fair-haired girl with her mother's smile, and her father's eyes and brow" (p. 372). Craik's narrator reproduces the colonial dream of the ultimate whitening of the dark(er) race through intermarriage with white colonizers, asserting the eventual victory of white civilization over non-white barbarians.

Such metaphorical rewriting of one's racial past was in line with nineteenth-century racial theories by which white settlers came to terms with the mongrel dynasties they themselves created. Relegated to the margins of society, mixed-race children were only reclaimed by the "centre" (England and their white parents) if they were economically successful.[1] In David Dabydeen's *Our Lady of Demerara* (2004), there are two major narrative voices: that of Elizabeth, an actress, and a descendant of Afro-Guyanese parents, and that of Lance

Yardley, a (white) theatre critic working for the *Coventry Herald*. Elizabeth's white complexion belies her family's mixed racial background, as "the only memory of an illicit past being the darkness of my irises and profuse black curly hair" (Dabydeen 2008, 14).[2] The use of the word "illicit" reverberates with nineteenth-century ideas about biological miscegenation found in the works of de Gobineau (1999), and still potent throughout the first part of the twentieth century in Europe and America. Even when interracial marriages were no longer forbidden, they were frowned upon by society, because they defied the black and white polarity (Berghahn 1977, 4–5). Elizabeth's body has obliterated the dark blood as it has been metaphorically "bleached" by white European culture.

However, contrary to popular stereotypes of white supremacy and black subservience, she is the rich heiress of an upper-middle-class background, while Lance is "white-trash", a poor underprivileged boy/man, with a family scarred by their past. His long lost mother who, according to his sister Miriam and various other friends, disappeared with a "darkie" (p. 38) when he was still a child, hovers as a vivid reflection of his rootlessness. Lance's search for her takes on both a literal as well as a symbolic meaning, co-related with his exploration of his own confused sense of identity. For Lance it is family history that beleaguers him, his father's periodic absences and his mother's permanent vanishing; whereas for Elizabeth it is her cold and withdrawn yet always present parents. Elizabeth faces the present predicament of her relationship with Lance; telling and re-telling their story she constantly eradicates the boundaries between truth and fiction. Likewise, Lance, in his attempts to reclaim the story of his mother, transgresses the limits of truth by fusing two archetypal images – that of the unattainable virgin and that of the all-too-available whore. Even the title of the book invites such ambiguity, as the "Lady of Demerara" can be read as an invocation to the Virgin Mary, but "our lady" can also signify a common woman.[3] Adopting the (post)postcolonial perspective, and bearing in mind Sarah Ahmed's claims about memory and estrangement (Ahmed 2000, 91), my interpretation concentrates on the characters' processes of re-writing/re-thinking who they are, in the context of ever-fluctuating racial, social, cultural and ethnic identities. The characters themselves can never be described as finite products; rather, they are emblematic of the course of reconstruction of identities. Thus, Dabydeen's dialogue with the past has to be seen within the larger framework of (literary) history, which is continually rewritten, and therefore is part of an ongoing process and not a stable product.

"For all our days are passed away in thy wrath: we spend our years as *a tale that is told*" (Psalms 90: 9), the Bible tells us. Contemporary theories of identity highlight the fact that identities are formed in and through the narratives that we tell about ourselves.[4] We repeat stories from our lives at dinner tables or during meetings with friends; our lives thus become tales told and retold incessantly as time goes by. Retelling is the very essence of contemporary literary practice, linked to the process of altering the critical perspective. Consequently, one of the tenets of postcolonialism has been the implementation of a new angle through which the Anglo-European perspective viewed other cultures, which in effect led to a reappraisal of the notion of Englishness. As R.J.C. Young claims, "Englishness is itself also uncertainly British, a cunning word of apparent political correctness invoked in order to mask the metonymic extension of English dominance over the other kingdoms with which England has constructed illicit acts of union, countries that now survive in the international arena only in the realm of football and rugby" (Young 1995, 3).

In the nineteenth century, approaches to identity were marked by binary oppositions of white and black, with the superior race being always invariably white, as in the words of Miriam, another of Dabydeen's characters from an earlier novel, *The Counting House*: "Whitepeople born different, eh?" (Dabydeen 2005, 114; original spelling). This intimation parallels that of one of the greatest racists ("racialist") of the nineteenth century, Arthur Comte de Gobineau, who argued for the historical, biological and religious superiority of the white race: "Adam is the ancestor of the white race. The scriptures are evidently meant to be so understood, for the generations deriving from him are certainly white" (de Gobineau 1999, 118).[5] In de Gobineau's vision of the world, colonial experiences are fundamentally racial experiences, but, more importantly, he indirectly stresses that everything is in the constant state of flux, be they great civilizations or racially inferior societies. Yet "the irreconcilable antagonism between different races and cultures is clearly established by history, and such innate repulsion must imply unlikeness and inequality" (p. 179). De Gobineau's nineteenth-century imperialist idiom suggests that hybridity is biologically undesirable, while, in contrast, early postcolonial theories saw hybrid identities as a way to link the colonized and the colonizers. As early as 1925, José Vasconcelos wrote his seminal essay *La raza cósmica* (*The*

Cosmic Race), in which he predicted the coming of a new age in Latin America, that of a mixture of the old and the new peoples, whose hybrid racial features will be regarded as new canons of beauty.[6] In more recent theories, hybridity is used in connection with second- and third-generation immigrants of mixed racial heritage, but also in relation to mixed cultural backgrounds of such immigrants born into families living in Britain and America (Pieterse 2007, Brah and Coombes 2000). However, both sociological as well as cultural theories such as Young's (2003)[7] warn against easy appropriation of the term, showing hybridity as in itself an unsteady, fluctuating phenomenon. In *Our Lady of Demerara*, as in much of his earlier poetry, Dabydeen constantly plays with these notions of race and hybridity by continually undercutting their theoretical basis and transgressing the boundaries of difference.

Since the nineteenth century, theories about race and gender were often closely linked. Herbert Spencer, the eminent biologist, saw non-white women as "lower races". "They were called innately impulsive, emotional, imitative rather than original, and incapable of the abstract reasoning found in white men" (Stepan 2002, 7). Not only did such theories belittle women, they first and foremost demeaned people of colour. In *Our Lady of Demerara*, Elizabeth is very much aware of the stereotypical binary opposition between black and white, and also understands that Lance is primarily fascinated by her because of the untamable and even savage element that he believes she contains. Dabydeen's novel toys with the analogy between racial and sexual differences so potent in earlier scientific discourse by showing the fundamental falsity of such analogies. What is crucial in Dabydeen's novel, then, is not only the fact that both Lance and Elizabeth are hybrid characters, but that both of them are searching for a sense of identity, for neither is able to find "identity" by simply "stepping into the past" (Dabydeen 2008, 91).

The theme of migration is closely tied to that of identity, and plays a major role in the history of Elizabeth's family, even though she does not have the experience of being an exile herself. Unlike thousands of immigrants to Europe, Elizabeth's family did not leave their homelands to seek a better life abroad, but felt, ironically, that they had returned "home" to England.[8] The novel is, of course, set in Britain during the 1990s, but Dabydeen undercuts the easy equation of poverty and non-European immigration to Britain[9] by making her family relatively well-to-do. In the nineteenth century, analogies of racial, gender and class differences had generated metaphors which shaped highly biased perceptions of immigrants to Britain. Instead of countering such traditions, Dabydeen plays with them and uses the potent image of the refinement process from brown sugar into white by correlating the whitening of skin with Elizabeth's family's increase of wealth:

> Sometime in the nineteenth century Indian blood entered our family history. My great-grandfather, a sugar planter in Demerara province in a country called Guiana, took up a local as his mistress, a young widow who had arrived on a coolie boat from India. A child was born, my grandmother, who married an Englishman. She was shipped off to a private school on the outskirts of Coventry at the age of eight, and ten years later, on the death of her father, she inherited a fine mansion there, a considerable annuity. My mother in turn was bequeathed the property and made a fine marriage to a local dealer in motor accessories. One day, all their wealth would pass to me, their only child. Over time, my family had increased and consolidated their wealth, in the process of becoming lighter of skin, *eventually reverting to our original colour* [my italics]. Like raw sugar, pungent in its brownness, becoming aromatic white through the process of refinement. (p. 14)

It is equally ironic, however, that Elizabeth is only interested in her past inasmuch as it contributes to her understanding of herself, her emotions and needs. Hence, the recollections of her great-grandmother who came from Bihar in India are inscribed within the context of Guyana's colonial past as "the English shipped thousands of them [coolies] from India to Demerara, to work in the canefields" (p. 14), rather than being emotionalized through images of poverty and desperation as her ancestors escaped from hunger and disease in their native villages.

Being disinterested in her family history, pretending and putting on various masks seems to be the way of life for Elizabeth, as she colours the reality around her. Writing to her parents before her marriage to Lance, Elizabeth ameliorates Lance's family members, making Miriam, his sister, a nurse, and his nephew honest and respectable, and "upping" Sarah's age to make her pregnancy more respectable (pp. 57–58). Despite her own privileged background, Elizabeth is somehow emotionally and culturally rootless and cannot find a place or identity for herself; she is initially a secretary and then an actress in third-rate amateur performances, only to then assume the role of Lance's wife, in which she is equally amateurish.

In numerous interviews, Dabydeen has frequently stressed his fascination with English literature, but while acknowledging its importance he nevertheless plays in his fiction with the concept of there being a "great tradition" of colonial writings. Thus, the character of Elizabeth could be read as an heir to a long line of literary characters, Charlotte Brontë's and Jean Rhys's Bertha/Antoinette Rochester being the most notable one.[10] She does have money, but, like her literary predecessors, instead of bringing her happiness it only affords purposeless emptiness.

By virtue of her hybridity, Elizabeth embodies contemporary ideas of multiculturalism which confront traditional hierarchies of wealth and power. Even though she is not specifically ashamed of her ethnic background, she never mentions any other members of her more extended family, as if the West Indian whitened line was the only one of importance.

Ethnicity is, of course, an unstable category subject to reinforcement and enhancement through the community in which an individual lives. According to Jan Nederveen Pieterse, "Ethnic identification is a matter of ongoing relational positioning" (2007, 32). He claims that "the logic of ethnicity is that of imagination, and imagination is that of social practice" (p. 38). Elizabeth's identity, however, is grounded in cultural practices of performance (identity as performance is stressed in numerous linguistic, psychological and cultural studies). She creates herself in and through the language she uses: "I was Elizabeth ('Beth' to Lance's kind, I resented the common abbreviation). I was middle-class, that was that, why bother to excuse myself? I even pitied Lance's obsession with class" (Dabydeen 2008, 14). Her ironic presentation of her visit to Lance's family as his father lay dying highlights divergent perceptions of reality: "Access to the scene . . . yielded little except the obvious: a childhood of poverty in a working-class or welfare-dependent district of Coventry . . . Lance's father, in spite of his decay, was a farcical figure . . ." (pp. 30–31). Elizabeth's character is thus formed within the discourse of gender *and* class, rather than race.

What is frequently stressed in sociolinguistic works on identity is the fact that human identity is an invention, and various narratives of the Self help to develop private self-perceptions.[11] More than Lance, Elizabeth is capable of narrating a relatively stable story of herself, but nevertheless her performances of self are often critiqued by Lance, who criticizes her life "drama" as much as he praises her theatrical roles. In a moment of self-awareness, Elizabeth admits: "I was a fake, lacking true and spontaneous warmth . . . *Upper-class twit, you only want to slum it with us, Albion Hill is a little underclothing excitement for you, that's all.* He was denying me entry into his world. After a while I grew tired of his outbursts. I accepted my status as a scion of privilege" (p. 43). Elizabeth's ultimate act of violence, of aborting of Lance's child (p. 46), is not only her final severance of her ties with Lance, but first and foremost an act of refusal to be written into the narrative of a particular family life, his family life. While stressing the luxury that money can buy, especially at an abortion clinic, she nevertheless sees herself as empty, rid of the future with Lance, and still lacking in any stable form of identity.

Elizabeth's past of financial security and privilege is then contrasted with Lance's family history, the family that for Elizabeth represent the underclass, the pariahs of the contemporary world: "Banal talk in a shabby council house with a set of semiliterate people of Irish breed, and the father dying without dignity" (p. 31).[12] This "Albion Hill" mentality is also built up through the racist remarks such as those made by Lance's father: "Kill the fucking nigger before the nigger fucks you" (p. 42). Superficially, it appears that Dabydeen is reinforcing the old maxim that lack of breeding always breeds intolerance and prejudice.[13] Their low-class poverty is seemingly presented through typical contemporary discourses; one is judged by the clothes one wears and the food one eats. In Lance's father's house, the inhabitants eat chips and marshmallows. Lance's mother "was accustomed to scraping together a living and surviving on potatoes. We were content with the second hand clothing Mum acquired for us from various charity shops. We never complained about the unvarying diet of grease she reared us on" (p. 28). The consumption of unhealthy food is the most visible sign of low status, yet Lance's and Elizabeth's stereotypically assumed class conflict is actually an ironic reversal of contemporary perceptions of poverty and affluence as constructed in and through cultural and racial discourses.

Despite the fact that Lance's family embodies the formula of poverty – a crowded house, junk food and teenage pregnancy – Lance seems to be proud of his low origins and uses his family as an instrument of psychological war with Elizabeth, contrasting their openness with her reticence. It is hardly surprising that Lance holds against Elizabeth the fact that she left him when his father was dying: "She should have stayed for Dad's death. I resented her departure, her not witnessing the drama of his final moments. She, an amateur actress in pantomime and provincial theatre, missed out on the universal drama of his going" (p. 41). Once again a woman had deserted him. Even the prostitutes to whom Lance had been drawn are not a constant presence in his life. Lance's world is forever marked by instability.

As a child, Lance was used to a one-parent family, and he and his sister knew what to do in case the police came to take his father away, collecting his things in a plastic bag ready for the prison. His last release, however, manifested the end of their childhood and the final searing of the family: "The day of his fourth release left me with an abundance of toys but motherless" (p. 30). Both Lance and his sister Miriam go through trauma of loss, but it is the uneducated Miriam who realizes how deep Lance's wounds run. "Lance is porcelain born under a bright star, but Mum turned him into mud didn't she, turned him into mud. Talk about a miracle! Jesus don't have nothing on her, our mum!" (p. 33). Lance's identity was unwaveringly blemished by the sordid nature of his family history, and the only way to deal with abandonment and absence was by filling his life with (hi)stories. For Elizabeth, however, he "would remain an Albion Hill boy, thwarted, unfulfilled" (p. 69). What she only half-understands is that his psychic trauma is an intense personal suffering involving a lack of recognition of the realities that contributed to that suffering. When Elizabeth finally abandons Lance and joins her parents in their Mediterranean house, Lance significantly begins his search for his mother. It is that desperate hunt for the feminine element in his life that makes Lance so hungry for women. As Samaroo, the owner of the shop in which Lance meets Rohini, says: "Lance . . . seeking in Rohini the virginity of his mother even as he entered and raged within her" (p. 109). Rohini, whose adopted name was that of the pastoral heroine, Corinne, is a prostitute, and her attraction lies not only in her girlish body but also in her unpredictability, her varied performances of the self. When she gets murdered, Lance finally begins to reconsider his past: "Writing a factual, and even forensic, mode made Corinne disappear as a person and made my sexual relationship with her a simple matter of commercial transactions" (p. 70).

For Lance, his abortive relationships with both Elizabeth and Rohini as well as his mother's stories trigger the impulse to re-think the events of his life, an impulse perhaps inherited from his father: "Dad must have thought it his duty to construct the family saga, giving them the details of their infant biographies, reminding them of later childish pranks and accidents" (p. 21). In a similar fashion, Lance (re)creates his own life in a narrative through which he wants to redeem himself: "December 20th 1991 – I have come to Demerara to find the priest in myself, and so be cleansed of sex" (p. 75). At first glance, his is the written confession. Yet instead of his life story we are offered a Lance rewritten into the life of an Irish priest who went to Guyana – coincidentally also the place of origin of Elizabeth's grandmother – at the beginning of the twentieth century. In this narrative, which Elizabeth receives in the form of a manuscript from Samaroo, she is cast in the role of the Irish priest's mother:[14] "The mother – I name her Beth . . ." (p. 133). Even before reading the manuscript she recognizes that "the world he [Samaroo] belonged to was alien to me" (p. 99), and Lance's world was equally alien to her.

By virtue of making the reverse journey of British, Indian and African immigrants or slaves, Lance is also re-writing the history of the Middle Passage and its thousands of nameless victims who passed away without being granted the privilege of having human identity.[15] Lance's journey can therefore be seen on a number of levels. First, the personal, where his aim is to counter his father's failures, and to reclaim the female element of himself in order to become a different man. Second, historical, with the goal of tracing and salvaging the life of an Irish priest, Father Jenkins, who left England in 1914 as a boy of sixteen or seventeen (p. 77), and whose whereabouts he wants to uncover in Guyana. Incidentally, the name of the priest reminds one of Edward Jenkins (1838–1910), whose novel *Lutchmee and Dilloo* (1877) was the first to highlight the plight of nineteenth-century West Indian coolies, thereby commenting on the nature of intertextuality and appropriation. In the novel, Father Jenkins's predecessor and mentor is Father Harris, whose name is reminiscent of yet another Guyanese author, Wilson Harris (b. 1921). Such references are clearly indicative of Dabydeen's dialogue with both the Guyanese and the English literary traditions.

Our Lady of Demerara can be seen as voicing the postmodern concerns with novels as linguistic constructions. Both Dabydeen's "Lances" are linguistic constructs aware of their own textual status: "If I repeated the words sufficiently, would the magic of association restore Corinne to the present?" (p. 251). Reproducing nineteenth-century narratives of "going native", Lance's narrative shifts the focus from conquest to closeness. Unlike contemporary postcolonial rewritings of such phenomena, Dabydeen is not changing the perspective of the Other, but, rather, with the help of the strange and the unknown which Lance finds in Guyana, he makes Lance transform himself into a different person.[16] As Lance begins to understand that the sexual urge is in fact his constant search for the mother, he wants to erase the sins he has committed from his conscience. The deep self-loathing that Lance feels is undoubtedly the result of his mother's desertion, so by writing her out of the life of the priest's narrative, he metaphorically kills her and eventually is able to "lose his own self" (p. 94).

His journey, therefore, is akin to those emblematic and allegorical passages of literary characters like John Lydgate's Pilgrim and John Bunyan's Christian.[17] All such characters undertake long and perilous quests and battle the three enemies of mankind: the world (Lance's coveting of worldliness and material wealth), the devil (the sin of pride) and the flesh (sexual sins), the last being most picturesquely described in *Our Lady of Demerara*.[18] However, unlike his literary predecessors who depicted their supposedly authentic experiences, Lance creates a fictional narrative. Rewriting the life of the priest as his own, he re-composes the lives of people around him. Contrary to psychoanalytical assumptions about the liberating value of truth, Lance does not find comfort in his own memories, but in the fiction he creates. In Samaroo's words: "It's a mystery to me but I suspect it's Lance's re-conception of his own life, his reincarnation if you like, though it purports to be that of a priest. He has secreted himself in the vestments of the Church. But no, maybe something more queer, a blending of his life with a priest, a kind of sacred marriage or master-slave wedlock" (p. 99). Annihilating the Albion Hill character, and assuming the personality of an Irish priest in Guyana, Lance builds the image of a truly hybrid post-national identity, where the elements of ethnic and cultural distinctiveness are inconsequential. Lance's passage to Guyana does not have the markings of postcolonial rewriting, but suggests an even deeper instability of the contemporary human self. Personal narratives are always based on "identity states", presenting discontinuous identities, whose traits change with time. Linking episodes as well as drawing on various sources – such as other people's memories of the same events – so as to uncover personhood, is therefore a necessary process of creation,[19] and this appears to be precisely what Lance is attempting to do.

The novel's formal structure – which includes the possibility of recombining elements of the past in which neither the world around nor individual identity is constant – is also a comment on realism, on writings such as Jenkins's. In a truly postmodern fashion, Lance – more than Elizabeth – is the questioning subject, transposed and turned from a drama critic into a Prospero, pulling strings and ordering his actors to become what he wants them to become:

> My priest's story was broken and haphazard. Cryptic lines. Gnomic paragraphs. Obscure notes. Doodles. Impossible puns. I would mend the sentences, make them flow, give them purpose and direction. I would design his life, and where there were holes and gaps I would conceive of incidents and themes. My landfill would be my imagination but I would draw too on actual people I knew, give them places in the story. Miriam, her children, my father, Geoffrey, Beth, Corinne – they live ordinarily, purposefully, even stupidly. I would revise their existence on the page, or originate a new existence for them. As for me, I too would subject myself to the alchemy of writing, hoping for some measure of renewal, some fulfilment of potential or else a complete transformation of self. The priest's autobiography would at times become mine, populated with my Albion Hill relatives whom I would resurrect in different forms so that hidden aspects of their character could come to light. Or if in real life that had no depth, nothing to be revealed, then I would reinvent them altogether. If, because of superior education, I owed them anything, then it was to rewrite them. (p. 93)

If this is perhaps an all-too-obvious conclusion concerning the working of personal and public memory, the above quotation demonstrates the very purpose of story-telling, and the way in which personal experiences are transformed into public (written/literary) discourse.

Lance sees Guyana as a colonial territory bleak with its history of murder and pillage, "a history of cross-breeding. Hindus, Africans and even the odd Chinese – traders, adventurers, runaways from plantations or from the city police – had passed this way . . . What was remarkable was the seeming harmony of this mongrel community" (p. 103). These "mongrel communities", as if subscribing to de Gobineau's views, are not capable of creating a new civilization, being forever suspended in a state of primal ignorance, their ethnic identity forever volatile, refusing to accept the contemporary rational world and desperately clinging to the old myths and beliefs. Lance is certain that the Arawaks killed Father Jenkins (p. 107), but has no proof (it was supposedly a Kanaima who "took" Father Jenkins), and once again history becomes a story, penetrated by myth and fiction. In the "New World", as was the case in Lance's own surroundings, life is marked by destruction and decay. What

Lance sees is not the very moment of apocalypse, but rather the result of the colonial past: "Famine. Plague. Wasteland. All creatures had perished except the miracle of a bird, the last, no, the first living thing in the sky which the archer would bring down out of spite for God" (p. 131).

So where is accurate history to be found? One way of searching for truth is to admit that it does not exist as one unified narrative. Instead it manifests itself in a multiplicity of narratives and it exists in objects: "Doorknobs suggest so much about history. The brass ones are best, especially when they're a little dented or the sheen has worn off. You find yourself meditating on all the hands which have turned the knob over years, decades, centuries even – and opened the door to wives, husbands, children – what greeting or rejection they received" (p. 25). History is then seen as an incessant life process, always mutable. In Lance's narrative: "He [Father Harris], born in 1840, would be given a few more years at the most; I, born around 1897, might go on, by God's grace, to the 1960s. Others would replace us, as we had replaced others" (p. 224).

The most striking feature of the novel is its assumed multiplicity of seemingly incongruous monologues, memory lapses and necessary omissions that often render the narratives incomplete. For the two major voices, those of Elizabeth and Lance, the ability to write about a past one no longer inhabits is, at best, a difficult task. Hamlet rewrites his family history in an effort to reach the truth, to enter the realm of forbidden relationships and understand his mother's wrong choices, and eventually to change the future. Dabydeen's characters rewrite themselves precisely for the opposite reason, to veil the truth and to change the past. Hamlet's tragic dimension lies in his entrance into the world of falsehood; Lance's and Elizabeth's writing/reading of "Lance's" story turns both of them into tragic heroes, who are denied access to the future. Nevertheless, re-scripting their genealogies, the characters confirm that all our lives are composed of stories. Rewriting is one of the fundamentals of postcolonial literature, as the former colonies write back to revision the past, to understand experiences of cultural exclusion. Only by locating themselves as speaking subjects of the past can they undo the trauma of colonialism, and in this way the new generations are granted a safe trajectory into the future.

Notes

1. Somerset Maugham's collection of stories *The Casuarina Tree* shows the nameless, mute and unclaimed mixed race-children. The story "The Yellow Streak" presents a grown-up whose greatest fear is that his mixed race will be discovered, and he will no longer be seen as legitimately white.
2. "Miscegenation" comes from the Latin *miscere* "to mix" + *genus* "kind". For a continuation of de Gobineau (1999) and a strictly scientific approach to race crossing, see Trevor (1953, 1–7).
3. "Common women" were women without husbands, and therefore belonging to everybody; the idea goes back to the Middle Ages. See Mazo Karras 1996.
4. See Eakin 2008.
5. De Gobineau uses various anthropological experiments, such as measurements of human skulls, to support his claims (pp. 106–16). Throughout the text, de Gobineau shows how the white race dominates the world (pp. 48–49), asserting that there are strong and weak races (p. xvii); he is very critical of the Hindu civilization, claiming that the Hindu people built for themselves only tombs (p. 91), and they "conceived a few ideas, which they did not take trouble to work out" (p. 92); he tries to do justice to the art of ancient civilizations, which surpasses (his) contemporary art. De Gobineau maintains that racial differences are permanent, but even the greatest civilizations cannot develop ad infinitum (p. 167) and the fall of civilization is an inevitable result of that constant upward and downward movement, evocative of the medieval Wheel of Fortune concept.
6. I am grateful to Dr Roberto R. Heredia, Professor of Psychology and Chair of Department of Behavioral, Applied Sciences and Criminal Justice at Texas A&M International University, for giving me the book and pointing to its importance in my discussion of hybridity.
7. "The use of the term hybridity to describe the offspring of humans of different races implied, by contrast, that the different races were different species: if the hybrid issue was successful through several generations, then it was taken to prove that humans were all one species, with the different races merely sub-groups or varieties – which meant that technically it was no longer hybridity at all" (Young 1995, 9).
8. Dancygier (2010) outlines the motifs for immigrant-native conflict, looking at cultural and political factors which lead to confrontation.
9. Stapan gives an example of "the 'poor of Europe' who are seen in terms strictly applicable only to the 'Negro' and vice versa. As a consequence, the poor are seen like a 'race apart', savages in the midst of European civilization" (Stapan 2002, 12).
10. See Charlotte Brontë, *Jane Eyre*; Jean Rhys, *Wide Sargasso Sea*.
11. For more, see Bucholtz, Liang and Sutton 1999 and Crawford 1995.
12. Lance knows that Elizabeth's decorum is put on, pretended, yet instead of severing

the ties with the family she secretly despises, he encourages Elizabeth's visits. As he sees it: "For all her curiosity about Albion Hill life, for all her kindness to Sarah and patience with Miriam, she could never gain access to our family, our past. Miriam sobbed when the doorbell rang and she called out our mother's name but I knew it was Beth come back, hungering for knowledge of our past which would always be denied to her" (p. 42).

13. What Elizabeth sees is the house crowded with people who simply hang out with the family, like Dave, who comes to take care of Lance's dying father, and says about his own mother: "She's like you lot, scrounging off social" (p. 16). Dave is not able to bring anything from the neighbourhood convenience store, as "Paki won't give no more credit" (p. 19). Elizabeth's observations confirm the stereotypes through which she looks at Lance's family: "Sarah would bear children by different men, or abort, her brothers would spawn bastards. They would behave towards each other with vulgarity and tenderness" (p. 62).
14. It is through Rohini's "friend" Samaroo, the owner of the shop, that Lance learns about the Irish priest in Demerara (p. 67).
15. For more on the representations of past and present representations of the Middle Passage, see Smallwood 2007 and Kowaleski Wallace 2006.
16. See Sarah Ahmed's discussion of the notion of going native in Ahmed 2000, 114–33.
17. John Lydgate, *The Pilgrimage of the Life of Man;* John Bunyan, *Pilgrim's Progress.*
18. The new Lance sees himself as innocent: "I was obviously aware of the existence of prostitutes from my reading of the Bible, but I was not privy to the details of their trade. I could know of them in abstract and general terms, but the particularities of their impure deeds were to be withheld from me" (p. 231).
19. For more, see Eakin 2008, 8–17.

References

Ahmed, S. 2000. *Strange Encounters: Embodied Others in Post-Coloniality.* London: Routledge.
Berghahn, M. 1977. *Images of Africa in Black America Literature.* London and New York: Macmillan Press.
Brah, A., and A.E. Coombes, eds. 2000. *Hybridity and Its Discontents.* London: Routledge.
Brontë, C. 2000. *Jane Eyre,* ed. M. Smith. Oxford: Oxford University Press.
Bucholtz, M., A.C. Liang, and L.A. Sutton, eds. 1999. *Reinventing Identities: The Gendered Self in Discourse.* Oxford: Oxford University Press.

Bunyan, J. 1987. *The Pilgrim's Progress*, ed. R. Sharrock. London: Penguin.
Caruth, C., ed. 1995. *Trauma: Explorations in Memory*. Baltimore and London: Johns Hopkins University Press.
———. 1996. *Unclaimed Experience: Trauma, Narrative and History*. Baltimore and London: Johns Hopkins University Press.
Craik, D. 2000. *Olive, The Half-Caste: An Old Governess's Tale*, ed. C. Kaplan. Oxford: Oxford University Press.
Crawford, M. 1995. *Talking Difference*. London: Sage Publications.
Dabydeen, D. 2005. *The Counting House*. Leeds: Peepal Tree Press.
———. 2008. *Our Lady of Demerara*. Leeds: Peepal Tree Press.
Dancygier, R.M. 2010. *Immigration and Conflict in Europe*. Cambridge: Cambridge University Press.
Eakin, J.P. 2008. *Living Autobiographically: How We Create Identity in Narrative*. Ithaca and London: Cornell University Press.
De Gobineau, A. 1999. *The Inequality of Human Races*. New York: Howard Fertig.
Kowaleski Wallace, E. 2006. *The British Slave Trade and Public Memory*. New York: Columbia University Press.
Lydgate, J. 1996. *The Pilgrimage of the Life of Man*, ed. F.J. Furnival. Woodbridge, Suffolk: D.S. Brewer.
Maugham, W.S. 1985. *The Casuarina Tree*. Oxford: Oxford University Press.
Mazo Carras, R. 1996. *Common Women: Prostitution and Sexuality in Medieval England*. Oxford: Oxford University Press.
Pieterse, J. 2007. *Ethnicities and Global Multiculture*. Plymouth: Rowman and Littlefield Publishers.
Rhys, J. 1982. *Wide Sargasso Sea*. New York and London: W.W. Norton.
Smallwood, S.E. 2007. *Saltwater Slavery: A Middle Passage from Africa to American Diaspora*. Cambridge, MA: Harvard University Press.
Stepan, N. 2002. "Race and Gender: The Role of Analogy in Science". In *Science, Race, and Ethnicity*, ed. J.P. Jackson, 5–21. Chicago and London: University of Chicago Press.
Vasconcelos, J. 1997. *The Cosmic Race*, trans. D.T. Jaén. Baltimore and London: Johns Hopkins University Press.
Young, R.J.C. 2003. *Hybridity in Theory, Culture and Race*. London: Routledge.

CHAPTER 9

"Everything Is Illuminated"
Trauma, Literary Alchemy and Transfiguration in David Dabydeen's *Molly and the Muslim Stick*

JUTTA SCHAMP

> How may son of dust find words,
> so pure, so light, so luminous,
> that they can rise up from the earth?
> – Strindberg, *Dream Play* (1962, 575)

IN THE LATE 1980S, WILSON HARRIS – one of the most important writers of the Caribbean – began to voice objections to a postmodern concept of art that reduces artistic self-expression and humanism to the ludic interplay of the signifier and signified, while ignoring the power of the unconscious and the intuitive (Harris 1992a, 58). To Harris, postmodernism was lacking in creativity and depth and did not have the potential to trigger psychological transformation and effect societal change (Petersen and Rutherford 1991, 30; also Harris 1992a, 22).[1] While David Dabydeen's work has often been analysed in the light of such postmodern (and postcolonial) theory,[2] this chapter will show the extent to which creativity and the "power of the unconscious" has been used to transform the lives of characters in Dabydeen's latest novel, *Molly and the Muslim Stick* (2008).

Similar to *The Intended* (1991) and *Our Lady of Demerara* (2004), Dabydeen turns his gaze towards both England and Guyana in *Molly and the Muslim Stick*. Tracing the heroine's open-ended quest for self-realization, the novel is set in a working-class environment in the North of England and the Demerara jungle between World War I and the 1960s. I will argue that non-linear *Molly and the Muslim Stick* amalgamates allusions to the works of Harris, August Strindberg, D.H. Lawrence, William Shakespeare, Joseph Conrad and V.S. Naipaul, and in so doing aestheticizes[3] and transfigures trauma and human suffering. *Molly* scrutinizes not only the paradoxical subject position of the colonized, but also Caucasian British masculinities, male violence, incest, nationalism, anti-Semitism, racism, Islamophobia and war. Relying on "creative cross-culturalism", the "unfinished genesis of the imagination" and taut "painterly" image clusters, the novel also explores the paradoxes, contradictions and ambiguities of Caucasian British femininities, their relationships with the colonized and, most importantly, the significance of transfiguration and personal transformation.

Weaving a Transcultural Literary Fabric

Trauma and transfiguration are key concepts in both Harris's and Dabydeen's aesthetics. To implement internal and external change, Harris – echoing C.G. Jung[4] – suggests facing one's mortality and revisiting the traumas one might have experienced in life to finally transform and, thus, transcend them. Harris calls this healing journey into the self "transfiguration": "On the other hand, finitude may make us aware that the difficulties we endure – the wounds we endure and have endured as far back as memory takes us – can become transfigurative windows into extra dimensions through and beyond our finite position" (Harris 1991, 27).

Like Harris, Dabydeen is interested in how to create beauty in the light of human suffering and catastrophe, caused by domestic violence, incest, the Holocaust or colonization (telephone interview; Eckstein 2001, 32–33). According to Dabydeen, Adorno's question of whether there can be poetry after Auschwitz[5] also applies to postcolonial writers. As a student and later on as an emerging scholar and writer, Dabydeen studied Strindberg's plays. Dabydeen notes, "I was captured by Strindberg's dream plays, his radical formal experiments, his actual attempts at alchemy, his sexual passion and disgust, the violence he did to himself [burning his hands in an alchemical experiment], and above all his final cry for transfiguration" (Dabydeen 2006b). Dabydeen was especially touched by the concluding lines of Strindberg's last poetic play *The Great Highway* (1909) (telephone interview), which portrays the autobiographical tragic main character, Hunter, reflecting on his unlived life and coming to terms with his mortality. In the last lines of *The Great Highway*, melancholic Hunter mourns his lack of individuation and implores:

> Bless Me, Your creature,
> Who suffers, suffers from Your gift of life.
> Bless me, whose deepest suffering,
> Deepest of human suffering, was this –
> I could not be the one I longed to be.
> (Strindberg 1962)

Although facing the tragedy of maybe never completely reaching their fullest potential or measuring up, human beings have the gift of coping with that challenge through self-expression and transformation in dreams (Dabydeen, telephone interview). Whereas some critics trace "transfiguration" back to postcolonial theory,[6] Dabydeen's use of the term has a strong spiritual-religious connotation, bringing Christian iconography and the author's academic background in art history to mind.[7] Pondering the representation of transfiguration in Christian art, Dabydeen appropriates and reconfigures this spiritual concept of transformation by juxtaposing it with Hindu images and defining it as "the movement away from darkness to light" (Dabydeen 1986, 47).[8]

The revolutionary power of finding peace through transfiguration and thus healing society is also hinted at in Harris's transcultural reconfiguration of traditions. According to Harris, liberating oneself from the shackles of the past implies re-inscribing the past, that is, going back to the multiple cross-cultural influences that have shaped a human being in a specific location, "uprooting" (Harris 1992a, 143), visualizing and recreating those traditions into something new. Partly relying on Jung's work on alchemy (p. 62), Harris calls this creative process the "unfinished genesis of the imagination".[9] Revisiting and reconfiguring the past (an ethnicity's specific histories, myths and symbols) through intuitive imagery that links the conscious with the "universal unconscious" is always an open-ended process (pp. 25, 62).[10]

Similar to Harris, Dabydeen's creative coping mechanism for the tragedy of humans' painful existence is the concept of *l'art pour l'art* (Eckstein 2001, 33). Harris's strategy of the "unfinished genesis of the imagination" is especially useful in enabling the writer to compose aesthetically complex literature through the use of sophisticated language (p. 34). Emphasizing the craft of writing, Dabydeen notes: "Writing is about the use of language like painting is about the use of paint . . . Writing primarily is about using words in a gorgeous, fantastic, bizarre way" (Dabydeen 2006a).[11] Echoing Harris, Dabydeen sees himself as an imagist whose symbols and metaphors should "say something in a way that has not been said before" (Dabydeen 2006a).

According to Harris, constructing a multi-layered memory through complex imagery includes not only local but also European elements. Instead of separatism and denying those European influences, which he calls "perverse cross-culturalism", Harris advocates a "*creative* cross-culturalism" (Harris 1992a, 41), which encompasses unveiling connections and interdependence between discourses, disciplines and ethnicities.[12]

However, being part of a transcultural artistic tradition and standing on the shoulders of literary giants might also pose a problem for young writers. Dabydeen laments with a twinkle in his eye that as a writer "you've failed already . . . you can't be Shakespeare" (Dabydeen 2006a) and bemoans, "Or how can you write the Guyana landscape in a better way or with more excellence than the way Wilson Harris does it?" (Stein 1999, 28). For Dabydeen, one way of dealing with the "anxiety of influence" is through alchemy,[13] which was originally the endeavour to transform basic matter into silver or gold. Following the anti-realist tradition of Harris, who appropriated the term from Jung for the literary self-expression of a writer,[14] Dabydeen uses the concept to highlight the creativity of the imagination. According to Dabydeen, the imagination allows people to overcome their suffering and trauma through their capacity to dream (Dabydeen, telephone interview).[15] In their dreams, people withdraw from "reality", and the imagination becomes the alchemist, transforming people's lives into a network of magical images.[16] Dabydeen is especially interested in what constitutes Caribbean alchemy. Focusing on "the theme of reversing, remaking or transcending history" (Dabydeen 1986, 47), Dabydeen explains that a Caribbean writer comes into his or her own through "writerly" cleansing and purification. Dabydeen compellingly conjectures: "The Caribbean artist is primarily an alchemist . . . The attempt at revising history imaginatively involves too the renewal or purification of conventional English imagery. The attempt at purification is not just a notional one but also stylistic and formal. But insofar as we always had this historic desire to cleanse ourselves of history, we found that we could only do that through the recreation of dream images and of original myth" (p. 47).[17]

Alchemy in David Dabydeen's *Molly and the Muslim Stick*

Building upon the oppression of Miranda through her father Prospero in *The Tempest* or Tess's selfish mother in Hardy's *Tess of the D'Urbervilles*, *Molly* probes the silencing of the protagonist's mother Maureen through her exposure to the abuse, wife battering and paedophilia of her husband Norman. The beginning of the novel is especially imbued with the realism of D.H. Lawrence's *Sons and Lovers*,[18] as well as the naturalism and deep pessimism of Strindberg's *Dream Play*.[19] The representation of the inexorable alienation and inhumanity of the mining pits and their impact on humans[20] echoes the drab working-class setting of England's North in *Sons and Lovers*, since hypocrisy, a double moral standard, anti-Semitism and Enoch Powell–style nationalism prevail in the "black and white" coal-mining town of Accrington (Dabydeen 2008, 27, 47, 113–14, 124–25, 136–38).

Maureen's husband Norman is a passive, daft, unimaginative and uninspiring miner who has accepted his poverty and shows little inclination to transcend the devastating effects of industrialization on his personality (p. 25). His lack of creativity is associated with dark colours, as well as basic food imagery, such as meat and potatoes (pp. 3, 22). During his marriage to Maureen, Norman becomes a predator, exploiting the misery of others.

Before her marriage, creative Maureen has dreams of a better life (p. 13).[21] Immersing herself in medieval romances that nurture her in her impoverished existence, she pictures her relationship with Norman as a genuine partnership (p. 19). In spite of her own humble background (p. 14) and in contrast to Norman's "illiteracy of the imagination" (Harris 1992a, 78), idealistic Maureen has the potential for transfiguration. Subsequently, she is determined to be somebody: "Promise you [Norman] won't ever give up on what's in my mind, and become nobody, and make me become nobody" (Dabydeen 2008, 20). At this point, the novel unveils the origins of domestic abuse and wife battering, since Norman knows that he is inferior to vibrant Maureen and that he won't be able to keep his promise to her: "He resolved to marry her, and with the authority that came with being husband of the household, he would sink her, pull her down to his level of being . . . He would make her surrender to his will, as she did earlier in their love-making . . ." (p. 20).

After the birth of Molly,[22] Maureen stops having sex with her mercenary husband, who starts preying on other women and his daughter (p. 24). Maureen fails to protect her daughter, who is associated with the image of a fledgling bird, threatened by a menacing black cat and craving a safe nest (pp. 3–4). Ignoring the incest, Maureen also fails to give Molly any affection or love (pp. 3–4). When Norman starts pimping his daughter to his neighbours from Accrington, Maureen withdraws more and more inside herself, loses her sanity, and is thus largely unavailable to her daughter (pp. 34–36).[23] However, in one of the few intimate and happy moments between her and Molly just before Maureen's death through the explosion of a bomb during World War II, Maureen is wearing a green dress – earlier in the novel green is associated with a happier life in the south of England (p. 13) – with red flowers, which Norman had bought for her when their relationship was in a somewhat happier place (p. 8). During Maureen and Molly's walk in the countryside, the narrator evokes Maureen's potential for *joie de vivre* and transfiguration: "I [Molly] remember her [Maureen] walking through the woods in her green dress – she resembled a plant which could move magically from spot to spot. I remember a green plant bearing red flowers gliding along the earth, entranced by its own wizardry, its freedom to move from this joyous space to that, no longer manacled by its roots" (p. 37).

It is Molly who will later on continue Maureen's incomplete journey to a fulfilling life. The colours red and green are an example of a Harrisian image thread that interweaves the characters in unexpected ways and highlights their unlived lives. Reflecting Harris's dualism, the colour red is ambiguous, since it does not only insinuate vivaciousness but also the violation of personal boundaries. For instance, in the opening section of the novel, the reader is introduced to incest and some of the core images of the novel, such as white light and blood. Remembering being raped by her father, Molly recalls: "The dripping down my thighs. Sticky, then thickening to treacle. As bloody as flesh from Leviticus. I lay awake listening to my bleeding, above the hog-snoring of my father who rested beside me" (p. 1). Reminiscent of the "pornography of Empire"[24] in *Slave Song* (1984) and *Coolie Odyssey* (1988), however, *Molly* also explores the complexity of abuse by making the protagonist not only a victim but also a perpetrator. As a consequence of the incest by her father and having serviced her father's friends, Molly manipulates her college friend, Terence, through sadomasochism and retaliatory sex (p. 57).

"Creative Cross-Culturalism" and the "Unfinished Genesis of the Imagination"

In addition to alluding to the richness of Near Eastern history,[25] Dabydeen also writes nearby and back to Shakespeare through the shape-shifting Muslim Stick.[26] Although Dabydeen notes that the novel's references to Shakespeare are just "semi-serious", "playful" asides (telephone interview), *Molly* reverberates with allusions to and reconfigurations of *The Tempest, Othello, The Merchant of Venice* and, to a lesser degree, *A Midsummer Night's Dream* and *Macbeth*.[27]

In contrast to *The Tempest,* which takes place on an island that is colonized by Prospero holding Caliban and Ariel as slaves, the colonial penetrates England in *Molly.* Stick is an amalgamation of several Shakespearean characters, such as the mischievous witch Sycorax,[28] the mother of Caliban who was banished from Algiers and had gained control over the island before Prospero and Miranda were stranded there. In addition to Sycorax, however, Stick also resembles rebellious Caliban. Whereas Miranda despises Caliban (*The Tempest* 1.2.348–51), Molly "marries" Muslim Stick, adopts black Guyanese Apotu-Om, and they form a closely knit family of outcasts.[29]

While Miranda prides herself on having taught Caliban the language of the colonizer (*The Tempest* 1.2.352–64), it is monolingual Molly who cannot follow the multilingual conversations between Stick and Apotu-Om (Dabydeen 2008, 99). She mainly relies on Stick, who understands Apotu-Om's language, which he believes is "a mixture of Sanskrit and a Greek dialect, but all in pidgin" and Aramaic (p. 92), and translates for her.

Stick and Molly's relationship is also suffused with implicit intertextual hints towards *Othello.* Echoing Desdemona, who falls in love with Othello because of his powerful storytelling (*Othello* 1.3.166–69), Molly enjoys listening to her multilingual Muslim "husband" Stick's stories about his travels through the Near East, Europe and the Americas from the Middle Ages to the present (Dabydeen 2008, 71–73, 75, 77–78). In contrast to male-defined Desdemona

(*Othello* 1.3.166–69), though, assertive Molly is reluctant to put Stick on a pedestal for his rhetorical skills (Dabydeen 2008, 78–79).

Similar to Dabydeen's *A Harlot's Progress* (2000), *Molly and the Muslim Stick* unveils and explores white supremacy, thus writing back to Miranda's unacknowledged colonialism in *The Tempest* (*The Tempest* 1.2.351–62). For instance, Molly wants to flaunt the enigmatic black Guyanese Apotu-Om on a trip to the British Museum in London (Dabydeen 2008, 108). Moreover, Molly, although eager to liberate Stick from bondage in England, has white supremacist fantasies in Guyana: "I hoped I was unique, that the natives had never seen a white body before and eventually might even worship me. I fancy being a deity. I miss being adored, handled preciously" (p. 164).

The novel also unravels anti-Semitism as a malleable construct and highlights the contradictions of white British identities. Due to her sexual abuse and exposure to pictures of the Holocaust, Molly identifies with the annihilation of Jews, but also recognizes her victimization as the origin of her own outbursts of anti-Semitism: "I started to dream of a concentration camp, a pen in which I was kept, a Jewess of your young age, and my father and our neighbours were my Germans . . . I tell you all this to explain why I loathe the Jew for she is myself, not even my shadow or twin" (p. 156–57). At the same time, however, Molly admits, "No, what was shocking was my outburst against the Jews . . . A Jew never set sight on me, much less laid his mind on me" (p. 156).

Molly also reconfigures anti-Semitic imagery through allusions to *The Merchant of Venice*. The narrator relies on explicit intertextuality when he refers to Shylock's "pound of flesh" (*The Merchant of Venice* 1.3.143–81), a fealty for the money Antonio had borrowed from Shylock, for one of the many women who had used Maureen's services as a clairvoyant but had also slept with Maureen's husband, Norman, by "giving her pound of flesh because the sex was pleasurable" (Dabydeen 2008, 32). Here the narrator practices image reversal by associating "pound of flesh" with the sexuality, adultery, selfishness and commercialism of non-Jews.

Moreover, Dabydeen re-imagines the representation of Portia and the Prince of Morocco in the casket scene. Both Molly and her friend and student Carol dislike Portia, and wish Portia had been more risk-taking and rebellious by choosing the Other, the Prince of Morocco, as her husband (p. 105), and thus question the construction of the obedient daughter. At the same time,

Molly – being complicit in Othering, since she is fascinated by the Moroccan Prince's origins in the "Hyrcanian deserts and the vasty wilds of wide Arabia" (*Merchant* 1.7.41–42) – calls Apotu-Om "Prince of Morocco" (Dabydeen 2008, 105). On the other hand, the narrator plays with gender constructions by making Molly the "exotic" prince in Guyana: "Think of my suitcase as the Prince of Morocco's casket, but full of things strange and fascinating to people here" (p. 147).

In addition to unveiling white British ambivalent feelings about Jews, the novel also investigates the paradoxical subject position of the subaltern. Muslim Stick, who presents himself as a transnational nomad with a multiethnic history, has anti-Semitic and racist traits (p. 101). Similar to Trinculo and Stephano, who get Caliban drunk (*The Tempest* 2.2), Stick's colonialism surfaces when he makes fun of Apotu-Om in a mock-baptism: "'Fetch another bottle,' Stick commanded. 'Let's tame the little savage properly, make him beholden to our beer, in thrall to our spirit'" (Dabydeen 2008, 102).

Transfiguration

The gradual transformation of Molly's suffering and despair is reflected in the reconfiguration of religious symbols. When Molly moves to Coventry, she puts a statuette of the Virgin Mary[30] on her mantelpiece; the narrator, however, partly cleanses this Christian icon of its colonial and religious aura, since it becomes the voice of Molly's supportive inner partner, encouraging Molly to continue her journey of self-exploration and expose herself to the unknown (pp. 87, 106, 169).[31]

Similar to Dabydeen's long poem *Turner* (1995) and *A Harlot's Progress*,[32] *Molly* also relies on *ekphrasis*, that is, allusions to Hieronymous Bosch's triptych *The Adoration of the Magi* (c. 1510). The central piece of *The Adoration of the Magi* depicts the Virgin Mary with the Christ-child Jesus in her lap and the three kings worshipping them. Discussing the visibility of blacks in European art history, Molly and Carol both associate Om-Apotu with the flamboyant black king in Bosch's painting and Christianity (p. 106).[33] Sensing the sacred in ordinary people and making religious art more democratic, Molly pictures Carol as the Virgin Mary in *The Adoration of the Magi* (p. 107). Inspired by Muslim Stick's autonomy, Molly "contaminates" the Christian symbolism of the Nativity scene even more since she decides to defy her hip injury and mold her own fate:

> Then, when it [decorating the Christmas crib] was done, by my own gladness and strength I raised myself, and as I did so I heard Stick moan, not in dejection, but in relief, for it was at last free from the burden of my wretchedness, free from the kingdoms of wretchedness which men had made of the world and my body. My hip would remain as incurable as the past, but no matter, for in this Christmas season I too would be reborn into a faith in the future. (p. 134)

Inspired by Stick's example of self-reliance, Molly's gradual transfiguration is visible in her increasing physical and emotional self-determination and independence (pp. 144–45). Having been an outcast in Coventry and subject to attacks by her xenophobic neighbours, who find her multicultural family of choice offensive, Molly follows the illegal immigrant Apotu-Om after his deportation from England to Guyana (p. 145–46).

The epistolary part 4 of *Molly* is the final chapter of Molly's self-representation, but could also be seen as a continuation of Carol's literary work-in-progress. Reminiscent of the metafictional elements in Strindberg's *Dream Play*, Naipaul's *Enigma of Arrival* or Shakespeare's *Midsummer Night's Dream*,[34] a meta-reflexive *Molly* playfully undermines a strict separation of reality and fantasy, and investigates the writing process. On the one hand, Molly's letters convey the immediacy of her experience in Guyana and thus add to the polyphony of the novel; the reader, on the other hand, cannot be quite sure whether Molly presents herself or whether her words are a product of Carol's or Om's imagination (pp. 169, 170, 174). Reminiscent of Wilson Harris's aesthetics, the blending of dreams and reality and the interlocking of various narrative Chinese boxes in *Molly* question objectivity and turn the novel into a narrative maze. Similar to Hisham Matar's epigraph about the transformation of Moses' staff into a snake, and the questioning of narrative authority in trying "to hold the tail/tale of anything and it vanishes" (p. iii), *Molly* undermines a linear, one-dimensional concept of reality and truth.

The last chapter of the novel especially underscores paradox and ambiguity by deconstructing the binary opposition of trauma in Britain versus prelapsarian, Arcadian Guyana. Guyana is not the place of carefree relaxation, since Molly is exposed to cyclical and cataclysmic Demerara mythology (p. 162) and learns about the colonial wars between the Dutch and the British

(p. 150), as well as the British missionaries trying to proselytize the locals (p. 162). In addition, she also hears about Apotu-Om's killing of a white missionary and intuits the colonization of Apotu-Om's village by people from Coventry (pp. 165–67, 168).

During Molly's trip on the Demerara River to find Apotu-Om's village (pp. 151–52), the narrator implicitly alludes to Marlow's journey in the Belgian Congo in Joseph Conrad's *Heart of Darkness* and dismantles both Molly's colonialist fantasies (pp. 59, 150–51, 171–72) and an openness to learn from the Guyanese (p. 170).[35] It becomes obvious, though, that Molly does not want to make Guyana her home, since she feels intimidated by the overwhelming presence and inexorability of the jungle (pp. 158–59). Similar to the piercing white light in Accrington (p. 1), Molly's intuition of past violence in the jungle is reflected in the bright light and the imagery of the fledgling bird. Reconfiguring the Christian iconography of the halo and radiance by associating it with the sexual abuse in Accrington, Molly exclaims:

> It was only a small opening in the trees, but the sun poured in as from a breached dam, so that when I sat away from the waterfall to dry myself my body was strangely lit. I looked at my arms and legs haloed as if belonging to someone singled out and blessed, and I remembered the first night with my father, the way the light had forced itself into my room, exposing me to his beak, a stone upturned exposing a gleaming white worm. I cupped my hand around that bird, believing it to be a fledgling fallen from its nest, but it was a crow crazed by hunger and would not relent until it was fed. (p. 160)

Being intoxicated from a potion by Apotu-Om, who wants Molly to see the hidden secrets of the jungle (p. 161), and afraid of becoming his prey, Molly feels threatened. Her premonitions don't come true, though, and – cleansing herself in the waterfall – she goes through a catharsis: "Countless mornings afterwards, having drunk the fortified golden liquour, Om led me to the waterfall. My initial terror was gone, I spent hours bathing and drying myself on the warm rock. Stick's anxiety too gave way to rapture as it rested beside me in the midst of mora and eucalyptus trees. Accrington receded into an unreal silence, its noises drowned in the swirl of water" (pp. 162–63).

Nevertheless, Molly refuses to marry Apotu-Om (p. 164). In contrast to Stick, who has found a home in the jungle, Molly is a go-between who feels that she can live neither in Apotu-Om's culture nor in patriarchal Britain: "I can neither stay here, in a primitive culture on the cusp of change, nor return to England which has yet to recognize women as equal to men" (p. 175). Emphasizing the importance of the river, the novel's ending combines Biblical, Hindu and Guyanese mythology. Similar to little Moses floating on the river Nile, Om prepares a Moses basket for Molly's journey. Subverting the ending of a traditional *bildungsroman*, the novel closes with Molly's continuation of her nomadic existence by embarking on a journey into the unknown, which might encompass possible spiritual rebirth, especially in the imagination and writing: "Curled up, covered from sight, I will float to wherever the currents take me. I will fall asleep and dream I am in my mother's womb, that when I wake I will be in the land of her promise, and in the alchemy of your [her student and writer friend Carol's] imagination" (p. 176).

The last paragraphs of the novel also celebrate the Hindu image of reincarnation and redemption through Stick becoming part of the eternal Demerara jungle: "I see a tiny sprig issuing from a crevice in its body auguring mongrel leaf and bud and flower. The Demerara jungle has embraced Stick in a new kinship and adventure into life" (p. 177). Thus the novel ends with a Romantic homage to nature and transfiguration, transcending time and even writing.[36] Molly predicts, "A thousand years after I've turned to dust it [Stick] will bear witness, as a living tree, to the love, to the grief, which stops us now from speaking words which have become needless" (p. 177).

Conclusion

Similar to Wilson Harris's works, David Dabydeen's latest novel *Molly and the Muslim Stick* is a tribute to the boundless power of the imagination, nature and the blending of Caribbean traditions with a Romantic aesthetic. As a literary alchemist who relies on the "aestheticizing" of trauma, "creative cross-culturalism", the "unfinished genesis of the imagination" and transfiguration, Dabydeen scrutinizes the paradoxical subject position and the ongoing journey towards the individuation of the white British female Molly. As this novel shows, for Dabydeen, it is the creativity of the individual that is the centrepiece of change. Reminiscent of Harris, Dabydeen notes, the issue is "imaginative liberation, liberation of the imagination" (Hand 1995, 79).

Acknowledgements

I would like to thank California State Universities Dominguez Hills and Northridge, as well as Santa Monica College, for generous travel grants and my colleagues for many inspirational conversations and support. My special thanks go to the participants (especially Brinda Charry and Alessandra Marino for their thorough reading and thoughtful comments on my presentation) and facilitators Jyotsna Singh and Gitanjali G. Shahani of the seminar "Shakespeare and the Postcolonial Condition" at the annual meeting of the Shakespeare Association of America in Washington, DC, in 2009. Last and not least, I am deeply touched by David Dabydeen's generosity in responding to my questions on *Molly and the Muslim Stick*. For their nurturing friendship and encouragement, I am extremely grateful to Cathy Moine and Christi Taylor Jones. For reading various drafts, I would like to thank Marie Barteld, Karin Yeşilada and, especially, Dolores Sloan.

Notes

1. On Harris's and Dabydeen's concerns about postmodernism, see Eckstein 2006, 167 and Dabydeen 1997, 135–43. Instead of applying Western theory to West Indian texts, Dabydeen astutely argues for relying on "a set of propositions about the history and culture of the region – a particular region [the West Indies], *derived from the body of creative writing itself.* The primacy of the writing must be restored, otherwise the centuries-old struggle for self-expression will be denied" (p. 138).
2. For example, Tlostanova 2007 in *No Land, No Mother,* the second anthology exclusively focusing on Dabydeen's work.
3. Compare Eckstein 2001, 31; also Eckstein 2006, 160.
4. Very thorough and succinct introductions to Harris's works are Hena Maes-Jelinek 1991 and 2006. On Jung's impact on Harris, see Mitchell 2006, 171–82, 281, and footnotes 21 and 22; also Harris 1992g, 62. In a telephone interview, Dabydeen told me he has never read Jung's works; however, he was exposed to Jung through Michael Mitchell's PhD thesis and book *Hidden Mutualities: Faustian Themes from Gnostic Origins to the Postcolonial* (telephone interview).
5. An insightful discussion of this issue; compare Eckstein 2006, 155–58 and Eckstein 2001, 31, 35; Dabydeen, telephone interview.
6. Hinting at Gayatri Spivak, Edward Said and Simon Gikandi, and discussing Aleid Fokkema's and Paul Gilroy's concepts of "transfiguration", Heike Härting distinguishes between "imperial self-transfiguration, plural and self-affirmative forms of transfiguration" (Härting 2007, 52; see 51–55).

7. On Raphael's *Transfiguration* (1520), compare Jodi Cranston's insightful essay "Tropes". Apart from analysing the central kneeling female figure in Raphael's painting, Cranston elaborates on Vasari's and Burckhardt's responses to the representation of the transfiguration of Christ on Mount Tabor (Cranston 2003, 1–6). Going back to Mark 9:2–13, Matthew 17:1–13 and Luke 9:28–36, "transfiguration" refers to the day when Jesus went with his disciples Peter, James and John to the top of the mountain Tabor. Upon reaching the summit, Jesus was transfigured, that is, his clothes became shining white, and Moses and Elijah appeared. Suddenly Peter, James and John were enveloped in a cloud and heard God's voice telling them to listen to God's beloved son Jesus. After this incident, Moses and Elijah disappeared, and Peter, James and John were alone with Jesus. One of the most famous representations of this incident from the Bible is Raphael's *Transfiguration*. Especially noteworthy in Raphael's painting is the stark colour contrast between dark and light: whereas humans occupy the lower part of his painting and are for the most part portrayed in dark, we see Jesus, Moses and Elijah in the upper half of the picture with Jesus in dazzling white (pp. 4–5).
8. In an interview with Lars Eckstein, Dabydeen conjectures: "I keep using the word transfiguration, I keep using the word redemption at the end of the day. Because I think all my work has been a kind of wrestling with Christian images, Christian images meaning the images that I grew up with as a child, which triggered off my interest in art, and then the Hindu images as well. I would say, at the end of the day I am much more interested in the idea of soul, an old-fashioned word like soul. I am much more interested in a kind of spiritual dimension, in a metaphysical dimension to art, than I am in the sociological, ultimately" (Eckstein 2001, 35–36).
9. Harris defines the "unfinished genesis of the imagination" as follows: "The balance, the creative and re-creative balance between cultures, requires an enormous penetration of tradition. It is a penetration of tradition which lays open tradition in a totally new way" (1992b, 112). On Dabydeen's concept of memory and the "unfinished genesis of the imagination", compare Eckstein 2006, 158.
10. Wilson Harris states: "We have a world that is tormented and torn and divided into all sorts of compartments, and the bridges between these cultures are very difficult to sustain. But they do exist. They can be found. They can be discovered and rediscovered, provided that there is a different kind of rhythm which requires us to read backwards and forwards, to read an image not simply in a linear way, pressing forward all the time, but sensing what lies behind that image, the way that image appears in a different context, the way it can open itself somewhere else" (1992b, 114).
11. This is reminiscent of Dabydeen's comments in Eckstein 2001, 32. Also Harris states: "my sense is that these imageries have within them an intuitive element which is peculiar and strange" (1992g, 33).

12. Harris notes about the construction of a multi-layered memory: "those archetypes, which they call 'native' archetypes, are all overlaid by European skeletons and archetypes as well. You will never activate them unless you activate the so-called 'European' skeletons as well. They are locked together and there is no way around that" (1992g, 40–41).
13. For a thorough introduction to the intellectual history of alchemy and its representation in transcultural writing in English (with a special emphasis on the Caribbean and Jung), see Mitchell 2006, especially parts 1 and 2.
14. On Harris's anti-realism, see Harris 1992c, 26; on Jung's impact on Harris's concept of alchemy, see Harris 1992g, 62. Talking about Penelope and her unfinished garment, Harris states: "It's the revisionary cycle which Jung identifies with ancient alchemy . . . Jung came close to suggesting a revisionary cycle. But he really never cared for imaginative literature. The result is that he always looked for the most banal fictions for his examples . . . And here one sees his genius in recovering these texts and bringing them back into play, as he did. These alchemical texts are, in the true sense, fictions . . . I came to [Jung] rather late and I had become involved in these things myself, but I was alone to a large extent. I had no one to turn to, and when I came to Jung and read what he had to say about the collective unconscious, it sustained and supported me. Because even then I was aware of intuitive truths arising from these depths . . . When I discovered the depths that exist in abstract ideas an afflatus came into my writing from what I would call the 'collective unconscious' of which Jung spoke. So I had a dialogue with Jung."
15. In Eckstein 2001, Dabydeen points out: "once you create space between you and a theme, you surrender it to the imagination" (30).
16. Focusing on writing *Slave Song*, Dabydeen states: "And one retreats from that world and attempts to recreate imaginatively images of a new romance (when you retreat from the real world, you can only live in a world of images)" (Dabydeen 1986, 47).
17. Dabydeen defines alchemy as follows: "In my own writing, Hindu concerns with purification and rebirth, which are part of my ancestral Hindu set of beliefs, are absorbed into the larger Caribbean obsession with cleansing and new beginnings. One could – trying to convert base metal into gold, even the mythical gold of Eldorado. The Caribbean artist is primarily an alchemist. This is not peculiar to the Caribbean. One finds the same literally as well as metaphorically in the works of Strindberg" (1986, 47).
18. Dabydeen has been intrigued by D.H. Lawrence's works for the evocative portrayal of the "ugliness of industrialization, the disgust with civilization", and his interest in the "Other" (telephone interview).
19. Compare especially the daughter's repetition of "Human beings are to be pitied" (Strindberg 1962, 533) and "Human life is pitiful" (p. 542), "Men are not angels, but

pitiable creatures" (p. 543), "life together is a torment. One's pleasure is another's pain" (p. 548) and "Poverty is always rather dirty" (p. 546).
20. Also compare Sandhu 2008, paragraph 1.
21. Note the similarities between *Molly* (Dabydeen 2008, 13) and the clothing-star imagery in the transformation of the tree, sky, stars and sun into Harris's peacock-palace: "The enormous starry dress [the tree] now wore spread itself all around into a full majestic gown from which emerged the intimate column of a musing neck, face and hands, and twinkling feet. The stars became peacocks' eyes, and the great tree of flesh and blood swirled into another stream that sparkled with divine feathers where the neck and the hands and the feet had been nailed" (Harris 1985, 112).
22. In a telephone conversation, Dabydeen told me that Molly is modelled after two people he knows.
23. Note the similarities between the description of Molly's bathtub (Dabydeen 2008, 36) and the ominous multi-sensory imagery in the following passage from Hardy's *Tess* (2003, 122–23): "The outskirt of the garden in which Tess found herself had been left uncultivated for some years, and was now damp and rank with juicy grass which sent up mists of pollen at a touch; and with tall blooming weeds emitting offensive smells – weeds whose red and yellow and purple hues formed a polychrome as dazzling as that of cultivated flowers. She went stealthily as a cat through this profusion of growth, gathering cuckoo-spittle on her skirts, cracking snails that were underfoot, staining her hands with thistle-milk and slugslime, and rubbing off her naked arms sticky blights which, though snow-white on the apple-tree trunks, made blood-red stains on her skin."
24. Quoted in Binder (1997, 168); also see Schamp (2008).
25. With Muslim Stick, Dabydeen also relies on Harris's aesthetics of making inanimate objects animate. Harris states about a realist description of a table: "It [the table] had a realistic purpose, a realistic immediacy. In so doing I was naturally tempted to reduce the world to convenient passivities and to enshrine a deprivation of the senses into tools of communication" (Harris 1992e, 72). On the other hand, reinforcing the power of the "intuitive imagination" and the interdependence of human objects, Harris conjectures: "the table comes from a tree in the forest, the forest is the lungs of the globe, and the lungs of the globe breathe on the stars . . . There was a more complex and intuitive approach to language in which one suffers and through which one perceives the peculiar ecstasies of dimensionality" (ibid.).

Elaborating on the intuitive imagination, Harris highlights the impact of Martin Buber: "According to Buber it was possible to have a dialogue with a stone. I understood that, as a surveyor. A stone belongs to a certain contour, a certain field. You tilt the field and the stone can be dislodged. Equally, when you see the whole globe from certain angles, your own prepossessions are dislodged . . . There is a language of the imagination which can penetrate self-righteous deprivation" (Harris 1992g, 62–63).

26. Dabydeen points out that a friend introduced him to the literary tradition of sticks coming alive (telephone interview).
27. In an online article, Dabydeen (2006b) states about the impact of Shakespeare: "Shakespeare was constantly present, a permanent hum in the air. He was a given, a certainty: it was a certainty that I could never write with his genius, so the next best thing was to try to achieve a few startling and original images and hope to claim a place even at the furthest edge of the great light he cast on literature."

    In *Molly*, there are very few allusions to Macbeth, but one is a quote from Lady Macbeth (1.5.17). Talking about Corinne, Molly mentions, "Not only was she beautiful but her breasts leaked the milk of human kindness" (Dabydeen 2008, 49). Echoing Puck's and Ariel's wish to be set free by Oberon and Prospero, respectively, in *A Midsummer Night's Dream* (2.1.146–47) and *The Tempest* (1.2.244–51), Dabydeen practices image reversal when Molly reflects, "Oh my Puck and my delight, I'll free your spirit soon" (Dabydeen 2008, 71). This is a turning point in Stick and Molly's relationship towards more equality.
28. Dabydeen, telephone interview. See *The Tempest* 1.2.
29. Molly describes her family as follows: "I was anxious to form a bond between the two of them [Stick and Apotu-Om], partly because they shared a language, but mostly because I longed for family. Stick, my peculiar husband; me, needing the chastity of our wedding; and now the boy-man [Apotu-Om] whom I would adopt as mystery and legendary child" (Dabydeen 2008, 94).
30. Dabydeen points out about his indebtedness to the Gawain Poet: "As to the Gawain poet, he gave me a sense of the sacred wrestling with the profane, love for the virgin Mary and lust for actual women, and life being an agonizing quest for both within the realms of the mundane and the magical" (Dabydeen 2006b).
31. Noticing the statuette's radiance, Molly states: "I looked up at the cabinet where I placed the Virgin Mary out of Cat's way, on the top shelf. The statuette was glowing like one of those novelty toys with a bulb in it. Except there was no bulb, the Virgin's skin was radiant by itself, like a figure summoned up by a séance . . . The Virgin spoke to me, pacified me, told me to follow Om. The Virgin told me not to fear the foreign, that she herself was widely travelled, appearing in India, Nigeria, Gibraltar; she'd been all over the British Empire. So there and then I decided to leave England, to renew my life overseas" (Dabydeen 2008, 148).
32. Dabydeen's interest in interdisciplinary approaches to art and *ekphrasis* is reflected in his doctoral thesis, *Hogarth's Blacks: Images of Blacks in Eighteenth Century English Art*; also compare Eckstein 2006, 117–76.
33. Elaborating on the flamboyant figure of the black king in the triptych, Molly imparts to Carol: "I explained the scene [*The Adoration of the Magi*] to her [Carol], dwelling on the figure of the black Magus. 'Isn't he just something! Studded with pearls, and look at the embroidery of his coat, so rich, with strange animals from another world.

Now that's what you call opulent, a figure worthy of worshipping the Virgin Mary. The other two Magi are plain and doddery beside him' " (Dabydeen 2008, 106).
34. Compare especially the scenes where the poet and the daughter discuss the importance of the imagination and the nature of poetry and dreams (Strindberg 1962, 573, 579, 585–86); Naipaul 1987, especially "The Journey", 95–179; Shakespeare, *A Midsummer Night's Dream*, especially 5.1.20–27.
35. This part of the novel echoes Equiano's ethnographic description of the Igbo in Nigeria in *Interesting Narrative* (pp. 32–45).
36. As Dabydeen suggests, the novel's ending reinforces "the future is green" (telephone interview).

References

Binder, W. 1997. "Interview with David Dabydeen". In *The Art of David Dabydeen*, ed. K. Grant, 159–76. Leeds: Peepal Tree Press.

Cranston, J. 2003. "Tropes of Revelation in Raphael's *Transfiguration*". *Renaissance Quarterly* 56, no. 1: 1–25.

Dabydeen, D. 1986. "On Writing *Slave Song*". *Commonwealth* 8, no. 2: 46–48.

———. 1987. *Hogarth's Blacks: Images of Blacks in Eighteenth Century English Art*. Manchester: Manchester University Press.

———. 1988. *Coolie Odyssey*. London: Hansib and Dangaroo.

———. 1997. "Teaching West Indian Literature in Britain". In *Studying British Cultures: An Introduction*, ed. Susan Bassnett, 135–51. New Accents series. London: Routledge.

———. 2000a. *A Harlot's Progress*. London: Vintage.

———. 2000b. "On Samaroo's *Tempus Est:* The Earliest Colonial Rewriting of Shakespeare's *The Tempest*". *EnterText* 1, no. 1: http://people.brunel.ac.uk/~acsrrrm/entertext/Dabydeen.pdf.

———. 2004. "Derek Walcott in Conversation with David Dabydeen". *Wasafiri* 42: 37–41.

———. 2005a. *Slave Song*. 2nd edition. Leeds: Peepal Tree Press.

———. 2005b. *The Intended*. Rev. ed. Leeds: Peepal Tree Press.

———. 2006a. "Interview". *Coventry Conversations*, 23 November 2006: http://coventryuniversity.podbean.com/?s=David+Dabydeen.

———. 2006b. "Writers Who Have Influenced Me". *Crossing Borders: New Writings from Africa*, 18 August, 2006. British Council: Arts/Lancaster University: http://www.crossingbordersafricanwriting.org/writersonwriting/daviddabydeen/writerswhohaveinfluencedme.

———. 2008. *Molly and the Muslim Stick*. Oxford: Macmillan Caribbean.

Eckstein, L. 2001. "Getting Back to the Idea of Art as Art: An Interview with David Dabydeen". *World Literature Written in English* 39, no. 1: 27–36.

———. 2006. *Re-membering the Black Atlantic: On the Poetics and Politics of Literary Memory*. Amsterdam: Rodopi.

Equiano, O. 2003. *The Interesting Narrative and Other Writings*, ed. V. Carretta. New York: Penguin.

Grant, K., ed. 1997. *The Art of David Dabydeen*. Leeds: Peepal Tree Press.

Hand, F. 1995. "A Talk with David Dabydeen". *Links and Letters* 2: 71–86.

Hardy, T. 2003. *Tess of the D'Urbervilles*, ed. T. Dolin. London: Penguin (originally published 1891).

Härting, H. "Paintings, Perversion, and the Politics of Cultural Transfiguration in David Dabydeen's *Turner*". In *No Land, No Mother: Essays on David Dabydeen*, ed. L. Macedo and K. Karran, 48–85. Leeds: Peepal Tree Press.

Harris, W. 1985. *Palace of the Peacock*. In *The Guyana Quartet*, 15–117. London: Faber and Faber.

———. 1991. "Some Intimations of the Stranger: Interview with Kirsten Holst Petersen and Anna Rutherford". In *Wilson Harris: The Uncompromising Imagination*, ed. H. Maes-Jelinek, 27–30. Sydney: Dangaroo Press.

———. 1992a. *The Radical Imagination: Lectures and Talks by Wilson Harris*, ed. A. Riach and M. Williams. Liège: Liège Language and Literature.

———. 1992b. "Creative and Re-creative Balance Between Diverse Cultures". In *Radical Imagination*, ed. A. Riach and M. Williams, 103–15. Liège: Liège Language and Literature.

———. 1992c. "Judgment and Dream". In *Radical Imagination*, ed. A. Riach and M. Williams, 17–31. Liège: Liège Language and Literature.

———. 1992d. "Originality and Tradition". In *Radical Imagination*, ed. A. Riach and M. Williams, 117–34. Liège: Liège Language and Literature.

———. 1992e. "The Fabric of the Imagination". In *Radical Imagination*, ed. A. Riach and M. Williams, 69–79. Liège: Liège Language and Literature.

———. 1992f. "Unfinished Genesis: A Personal View of Cross-Cultural Tradition". In *Radical Imagination*, ed. A. Riach and M. Williams, 91–102. Liège: Liège Language and Literature.

———. 1992g. "Wilson Harris Interviewed by Alan Riach". In *Radical Imagination*, ed. A. Riach and M. Williams, 33–65. Liège: Liège Language and Literature.

———. 1999. *Selected Essays of Wilson Harris: The Unfinished Genesis of the Imagination*, ed. A.J.M. Bundy. London: Routledge.

Henderson, D.E. 2006. *Collaborations with the Past: Reshaping Shakespeare Across Time and Drama*. Ithaca: Cornell University Press.

Macedo, L., and K. Karran, eds. 2007. *No Land, No Mother: Essays on David Dabydeen*. Leeds: Peepal Tree Press.

Maes-Jelinek, H., ed. 1991. *Wilson Harris: The Uncompromising Imagination*. Sydney: Dangaroo Press.

———. 2006. *The Labyrinth of Universality: Wilson Harris's Visionary Art of Fiction*. Cross Cultures: Readings in the Post/Colonial Literatures in English series, 86. Amsterdam: Rodopi.

Mitchell, M. 2006. *Hidden Mutualities: Faustian Themes from Gnostic Origins to the Postcolonial*. Cross Cultures: Readings in the Post/Colonial Literatures in English series. Amsterdam: Rodopi.

Naipaul, V.S. 1987. *The Enigma of Arrival*. New York: Alfred A. Knopf.

Petersen, K.H., and A. Rutherford. 1991. "Some Intimations of the Stranger: Interview with Kirsten Holst Petersen and Anna Rutherford". In *Wilson Harris: The Uncompromising Imagination*, ed. H. Maes-Jelinek, 27–30. Sydney: Dangaroo Press.

Sandhu, S. 2008. "Wisdom of Wood". *Daily Telegraph* 3 March 2008: http://www.telegraph.co.uk/arts/main.jhtml?xml=/arts/2008/03/29/bodab129.xml.

Schamp, J. 2008. "'Written on the Body': The Re-inscription of Shakespeare's *Tempest* and *Othello* in David Dabydeen's *Slave Song, Coolie Odyssey* and *The Intended*". In *Texting Culture Culturing Texts: Essays in Honour of Horst Breuer*, ed. A. Müller-Wood, 109–45. Trier: Wissenschaftlicher Verlag Trier.

Shakespeare, W. 1997. *The Riverside Shakespeare*, ed. G.B. Evans, et al. 2nd edition. Boston: Houghton Mifflin.

Stein, M. 1999. "David Dabydeen talks to Mark Stein". *Wasafiri* 29: 27–29.

Strindberg, A. 1962. *Plays*, trans. E. Sprigge. Chicago: Aldine.

Tlostanova, M. 2007. "A Permanent Transit: Transgression and Metamorphoses in David Dabydeen's Art". In *No Land, No Mother: Essays on David Dabydeen*, ed. L. Macedo and K. Karran, 86–105. Leeds: Peepal Tree Press.

Williams, M., and A. Riach. 1991. "Reading Wilson Harris". In *Wilson Harris: The Uncompromising Imagination*, ed. H. Maes-Jelinek, 51–69. Sydney: Dangaroo Press.

Zabus, C. 2002. *Tempests after Shakespeare*. New York: Palgrave.

CHAPTER 10

The Magic of Your Making
Magic and Realism in David Dabydeen's Recent Fiction

MICHAEL MITCHELL

SOMETHING HAS DEFINITELY HAPPENED to David Dabydeen's novels. But, as with many processes of change that are gradual and consistent, it is hard to say what has taken place or when a significant difference can be observed. The signs are there, though, that publishers and readers alike have been unsettled, unsure what to make of his latest fictions, *Our Lady of Demerara* (2004) and *Molly and the Muslim Stick* (2008). *Our Lady of Demerara* went through a number of manuscript revisions before its eventual publication by the tiny Dido Press, evidence of significant differences of opinion between Dabydeen and his previous publishers, while *Molly* appeared as part of Macmillan's Caribbean series, rather than with a mainstream British imprint. This chapter will consider how these latest novels might be approached to take account of their brutally realistic elements on the one hand – a murderous obsession with prostitutes in one and serial child abuse in the other – as well as aspects that have been described as absurdist or fantastic, like a talking Muslim stick. In particular, I would like to consider whether they can usefully be described within a tradition of magical realism.

There is a sense in which these later novels become possible because the earlier ones have "cleared space" by refusing to allow themselves to be co-opted into any kind of grand narrative; just as Mungo in *A Harlot's Progress* (1999) refuses to allow Mr Pringle to determine what his stories should be, or *The Counting House* (1996) refuses to allow the commodification of either suffering or moral rectitude. *Disappearance* (1993) is perhaps even more radical in denying the very basis of realism itself, leaving only a tantalizing fabric of allusive and contradictory storytelling from which stable character, determinable narrator and recoverable plot turn out to be absent. If readers are to be so thoroughly disoriented in their preconceptions and expectations, deprived of the usual structures and sea-walls to protect them from the surges of the unconscious, it would hardly be surprising if they did not question the demands of the fictions on their attention. One online reviewer found *Molly*: "an equal combination of frustrating and appalling, and I hope it's the worst thing I'll ever read by Dabydeen" (Valere 2008), after an initial reaction in an earlier blog post that: "it (so far) is a well-told story of a case of sexual abuse from several angles". The inescapable conclusion is that the eventual disappointment was connected to the initial expectations of a realist case study. Wyck Williams, on the other hand, recognizes that it is the element of story that is most important, the author in league with narrator and characters: "When it's all over – in a giddy swirl of finale imagery – you might think: how extraordinary! Molly and her creator working their prose off in an art house of intricate fiction: inviting you to marvel at a curious case of female self-absorption" (Williams 2009). While the reviewer is aware that not everyone will be convinced by the character of Molly, his personal conclusion about the story is entirely positive: "You could say, for instance, you consider *Molly and the Muslim Stick* a bloody marvellous book. And that with all its subtextual moanings & heavings, the grim, incredible sex, you had a bloody marvellous, uprumptious time with it. Molly for one would be pleased to hear you say that" (ibid.). Kevin Davey, in a review of *Our Lady of Demerara* in comparison with Lawrence Scott's *Night Calypso* in *Tribune*, wrote: "Read *Night Calypso* if you'd like to know where black writing in Britain is coming from. But turn to Dabydeen if you want to know where it could and should be going" (Davey 2004, 22).

Our Lady of Demerara begins with an apparently realistic narrative, programmatically entitled "Abortions" and "The Old Testament".[1] The real world here is not only an abortion in the relentless sense of hopelessness conveyed in the depiction of a faceless suburb of a midland town and its inhabitants, but also in the central relationship between aspiring journalist Lance and slumming bourgeois actress Beth, which leads through abortive attempts to find fulfilment in sex to a literal abortion. One is tempted to see this part as a satire on the "comedy of manners" expectations of much mid-twentieth-century British fiction. Its centre of interest even teasingly purports to be a murder mystery surrounding a murdered prostitute. The theme of obsessive sexual consumerism is never far from the surface, indicating a constant tension between animal lust and the potentialities of consciousness:

> The beginning of a relationship was always the most pleasurable, the sheer self-indulgence in the other's flesh. Hour upon hour, days and nights of plundering, before the inevitable exhaustion, the inevitable boredom. Thereafter human emotions took over, the awakening of conversation, the unveiling of the other's character, the discovery of flaws, the flow of compassion, the making of tacit agreements to ensure a tolerable relationship . . . The sex would be mannered, for consciousness of the other's personality would rein in the desire for swift brutish triumphant orgasm. (Dabydeen 2004, 17)

Dabydeen highlights a cultural and spiritual malaise symptomatic of undiscussed and unresolved complexes which have surfaced with a vengeance to the degree that spiritual formulas and faith have lost their power, thus prompting Lance's search in Guyana: "I have come to Demerara to find the Priest in myself, and so be cleansed of sex" (p. 75).

Lance's journey is not primarily prompted by fear of police questions in the wake of Corinne's murder, or the meeting with Corinne/Rohini itself – which is as devoid of redemptive power as the relationship is mutually exploitative – or motivated by her uncle Samaroo's introduction to the wealth of Hindu traditions, although they begin to make clear that the uncoupling of language from what is held to be the real is both their weakness and strength: "The epitaph is exquisite, whereas the individual may have been a despicable creature. Is the language therefore fake or should we not simply marvel over it and disregard the character of the corpse? Our Gita dwells on such mismatch between word and flesh" (p. 64). Rather, it is the gift of the manuscript that draws Lance to follow in the "Priest's" footsteps and to reconstruct a manuscript which Samaroo describes as a "curate's egg", a jigsaw with unmatching pieces, a mixture of the sacred (the priest's hand) and the profane (the grocer's notepaper), a text "dense with puns" giving equal validity to incongruous opposites. Samaroo's gift recalls a lecture Dabydeen gave in which he described the finding of a reworking of Shakespeare's *The Tempest* called "Tempus Est" by an obscure Guyanese, also coincidentally called Samaroo

(Dabydeen 2000). In this lecture, Dabydeen asserts "the primacy of the imagination over race, class, gender, nationality and ideology", of the poetic imagination represented by Blake over the Newtonian "single vision" which leads to exploitation of the human and natural world.[2]

Lance goes to Demerara in search of "some form of cleansing" (at the age when Christ began his ministry) and arrives twenty-five miles upriver from Georgetown at the Mariella settlement. Mariella, of course, is the name of the place from where Donne's crew set off on their seven-day journey to the waterfall in Wilson Harris's *Palace of the Peacock* (1960). It should not be forgotten, however, that Harris's hint of redemption comes at the end of a second journey and after a second death overlaying the first, in what might be seen as a quantum or parallel reality, not as part of a linear process. So Lance's search, quickly abandoned in the dilapidated poverty of Georgetown, is also frustrated at Mariella, where the Indian Manu presides over a shop-cum-brothel where the pork-knockers, or gold-seekers, come for sexual relief: "'All-body here is foul, we is one spirit, no high or low, top or down, all is thief or abductor or buggar-man,' Manu said" (Dabydeen 2004, 79). From Manu, Lance receives a revelation of a different sort: the secret of organic process that makes up the natural world, a cycle of generation, parasitism and ruinous decay. Manu shows him how Hindu spirituality is integrated within this cycle: "We is Hindoo folk, we believe when we dead we turn into cat or crocodile or centipede . . . Whenever toucan settle on the crown of mora tree, I know is me dadee I seeing" (p. 87). The writer, however, does not seem to be presenting this as some kind of ecological Eden. Lance's disgust with Guyana, as expressed in a letter to Elizabeth, is associated with a description of a cockroach being eaten by ants.

What does become clear in this part of the book is the doubleness of everything, in which certainties, and thus the biases of individual identities, consume themselves in a play of opposites. Manu (meaning "lawgiver" in Hindi), is in fact Rajah ("prince"), who has borrowed his father's name for convenience. Lance is phallic weapon but also a seeker of the Grail. The Arawak woman (another allusion to *Palace of the Peacock*) is both whore and muse, and the Arawak village she leads Lance to is just a collection of huts. The mythic upriver Eldorado of Pillar is only a place where murder has been committed. Yet it also forms an allusion, being the last scrawled entry with variations like "rape" and "pillage" in the notes Lance has been given by Samaroo, establishing their provenance as Kurtz's notes from Conrad's *Heart of Darkness* (1899). The Arawak woman's pawpaw fruit seems also to be a chalice of gold and the juice like egg yolk suggestive on her body. The second half of the book, which Samaroo presents to Elizabeth like a child as Marlow might have presented Kurtz's last words, purports to be the recreation of a shattered eggshell of a story (one of a number of egg images used), in which the yolk or gold of transformation has leaked or secreted itself into the stories, while the reader is told that the lens, the way of seeing, is essential to the process of reading it. This is just as well, because the vertiginous indeterminability of the other elements of the story is thoroughly disorienting. The curious effect of this is described by Wilson Harris in his essay "Harlequin and Psyche":

> It is the alchemization of, or paradoxes of vision into, evolutionary layers blind in themselves, that one needs to turn and face in inmost self-reflection. That alchemization subtly disrupts the carapace or code within the miraculously perceiving self, miraculously perceptive human animal. That very alchemization makes for discontinuity within territorial imperatives – within "totalitarian" models of instinct – that begin, therefore, to mutate in the depths, even as they open themselves to the heights, and to innovate dialogue amongst parts of an unfathomable whole. (Harris 1983, 86)

In other words, redemption is achieved through the perception of the reader, not the fate of the characters.

Doubleness and ambivalence also characterize the story of Perseus and Andromeda, one of those which the narrator repeats to his grandfather in the second half of the book. Although he identifies with Perseus flying down on Pegasus, the winged horse of poetry, to rescue the damsel in distress, or threatened innocence, he is also aware of the erotic fascination of her bondage. The monster which threatens her, on the other hand, is also filled with sadness at its condition, and the damsel desires to be taken to the bottom of the lake by the monster rather than to be rescued by the knight with the Gorgon's head. It is a modernist situation explored in detail by Georges Neveux in *Le Voyage de Thésée* (1940) (made into an opera, *Ariane* [1958], by Bohuslav Martinu), about Ariadne, Theseus and the Minotaur, in which Theseus recognizes himself in the monster (and the monster in himself).

As Samaroo points out, it is the imagery and its lyricism which distinguishes the second part of the story (entitled "Reincarnations" and "The New Testament"), firstly from the notes of which it is supposedly composed, but also from the first half that is supposedly transformed and redeemed by the second, which in fact precedes it, although its transformation into a complete story is part of the first. The effect is to make both halves thoroughly dependent on each other. Thus, characters in the first part share names with others in the second, but do not always bear much relation to them. Direct comparisons do not so much produce echoes as harmonics and assonances. It would go beyond the boundaries of this short study to analyse them in detail. Lance, Elizabeth (Beth), Manu, Geoff, Arthur, Sarah, Corinne and Enoch are all names used in both parts, continuing a practice which Dabydeen has used in previous novels and continues in *Molly*. Two new characters appear in the second half, however: Father Wilson and Father Harris. These bickering adversarial twins, besides being wonderfully drawn comic characters, obviously carry programmatic resonance and announce a serious intention (indicated in the Harris quote above) which the postmodern indeterminacy and sense of play might seem to deny. It is therefore worth looking at their role in more detail.

Father Harris is the narrator's "mentor" in this second part; more than that, the narrator claims that he has "a dishevelment of notes" comprising the incidents in the priest's life, which he is now supposedly turning into a complete story. (Thus even the frame story contains inconsistencies and contradictions.) It is Father Harris who teaches the narrator to piece together the fragments of eggshells in his writing class:

> It was my task to match fragments as best I could, if necessary chipping away at them to form compatible edges, glue them together with utmost concentration, then paint them according to my own mood. "Don't cover over the cracks," he chided me when I presented the first egg to him, gloriously rounded and purple, awaiting his approval . . . "Always leave a memory of the original," he taught me when I re-presented him with the egg, pressing a finger into the top to open up a ragged hole. "The memory of the original only comes when you see the breakage, do you understand, boy?" (Dabydeen 2004, 159)

The process described here corresponds fairly exactly with the construction of the story itself, and is analogous to the comments he makes on Father Wilson's stuffed bird: "When it's alive you see the visible, if that, through glass eyes, because that's the way most of us are, glass-eyed. We only see the visible. It's the artist, the one who dreams oddly but whose waking life is an effort to clarify the dream, who knows the nature of the bird's particular livingness, even in its seeming dead state" (p. 178). This statement is framed by two further allusions: Father Wilson claims that "A bird is a bird is a bird", while Father Harris ends his remarks by breaking a pipe. The creed of realism is juxtaposed with surrealism's questioning of both representation and the idea of reality itself: "*Ceci n'est pas une pipe.*"

It is also worth considering the description of Father Harris's study, and particularly his books. It is not the Bibles he possesses, which are seldom used and seem to be different in their messages for each individual, that he wants the narrator to read and learn from, but an eclectic library of myth, science, poetry and anthropology, in which two elements predominate: the foundations of materialist and reductionist science (in Newton and Darwin) jammed up against the representatives of alchemy and the Gnostic/Hermetic tradition in Blake, Bruno, Dee and Agrippa.[3] The library indicates a preoccupation with the relationship between realism and the world of magic, beginning in a time when these were not regarded as incompatible.

The use of magical events in *Our Lady of Demerara* remains subtle and inconspicuous. The first occasion is Geoff's story of having been tricked by a man named Arthur into exchanging his car for magic seeds, which later sprout as fish. This is immediately associated with the folk tale of Jack and the Beanstalk, one of the stories the narrator of the second part has to tell his grandfather. It also reappears when Lance is in Guyana and is associated with Arawak legends about giant creatures beyond the clouds. In this story of an exchange that appears to be robbery in the real world but which gives access to a different, magical world offering ambivalent contact with opportunity and danger, there is a key to the redemptive possibilities of art and imagination. The Arawak woman, whose bracelet of beetle-wings recalls Shakespeare's Queen Mab, has the lined face of age and the immature breasts of youth, and stands in for the perennially absent mother of Dabydeen's fiction as well as the corrupted lover, but also the Muse who, Lance believes, will help him to "subject himself" to the "alchemy of writing". The story of the magic fish is treated with ironic scepticism in this first part, as Geoff is dismissed as "a right spanner" who "lives in the Mental" (p. 16), but is taken seriously in the punning logic of the novel as a whole, giving rise to a number of fish images, for example in descriptions of people in Father Harris's parish of Falmouth as having "slippery lives", "not taking the bait of doctrine", but who die "in a shoal" and who Father Harris buries in "allotments" similar to the place where Geoff's seeds had sprouted (p. 181ff.).

Towards the end of the book, odd events multiply, first in association with Alice, Father Harris's Falmouth housekeeper, whose oral inarticulateness is accompanied by written fluency and uncanny intuition, but who Benji the grocer claims to have confined within a magic chalk circle; with Miriam, who claims to have been attacked by a black monster and whose legs are turning into a tree; and finally with Corinne, and with Enoch, who pursues her.

In the figure of Enoch, Dabydeen has added to the gallery of mysterious angelic figures in recent fiction, joining, among others, Matty in William Golding's *Darkness Visible* (1979), Gibreel Farishta in Salman Rushdie's *The Satanic Verses* (1988) and Mr Verceuil in J.M. Coetzee's *Age of Iron* (1990). Father Harris compares Enoch with "Biblical Enoch", who uses convolutions of speech to mystify the ordinary and thus forms the opposite pole to Cardinal Newman, who Father Harris describes as a devourer of sham. The Enoch of apocryphal tradition is transitional between human beings and angels, and can be seen as an attempt to integrate the supernatural and the natural world.[4] In his study *The Demon and the Angel: Searching for the Source of Artistic Inspiration*, Edward Hirsch traces the angel as it appears in the Enochian sources, in Rilke, and in Klee, and relates it to Lorca's duenna, showing how they are two sides of what Yeats called the daimon: "the divine and magical inner self, an occult self that is even older than the body, is the origin of all Gnosticisms – Jewish, Christian and Islamic – and the crucial source for the hermetic corpus"[5] (Hirsch 2002, 61). It is also connected to Walter Benjamin's famous remarks on Klee's *Angelus Novus* from his "Theses on the Philosophy of History" (1940). Hirsch writes about Klee's paintings *Daemon* and *Angel, Still Ugly*: "We can't tell in either painting whether we are looking at one figure or two, and we can't distinguish where one figure ends and another commences. The self and the shadow-self, its anti- or antithetical self, are completely interlocked. Klee was following the etymology of the word daemon back to its root in daimonai, meaning 'divide'. His daemon, like his angel, is partly human, partly inhuman. And the artist is struggling to free his occult or immortal self" (p. 144f.). This description might apply equally well to Dabydeen's narrative technique, and Enoch becomes the presiding genius of both parts of the book, likened by the narrator to "the common thief who stayed awake for Christ's dying, under a sky jewelled with stars, so that having borne witness to the miracle of grace, he too could depart in peace"⁶ (Dabydeen 2004, 278, echoing 110) – a faith in the face of death (for he does not bear witness to the resurrection) for which Lance has been searching in the first part. Hirsch goes on to trace the demon/angel syzygy in the paintings of Mark Rothko, particularly the dark paintings of the Rothko Chapel: "Rothko's darkest paintings have the aura of the sacred, the immanence of a revelation, the promise of a secret that is always just about to be disclosed" (Hirsh 2002, 179). This quality is something that has now entered Dabydeen's work. One might recall the short story "The Painterboy of Demerara" (Dabydeen 2006), in which Dabydeen envisions a black assistant to a Hogarth transported to the Caribbean and completing a painting in shades of black (exactly as Rothko did).

The comparison with visual art is also relevant in the predominance of the visual in the second part of *Our Lady of Demerara*. Even the stories of Jack and the Beanstalk and Perseus and Andromeda, which the narrator has to repeat to his grandfather, are based on illustrations, and it is perhaps the plasticity of the storytelling which makes the work so vivid and memorable. For the stories themselves do not lead to a desired revelation. They should be read in a non-linear way, intertextually, each as a palimpsest of the other and in different dimensions, like the "worm-hole" readings Father Harris encourages his pupil to engage in to become "other wise" (Dabydeen 2004, 227). They are stories which leak out of characters at the least prompting, or which the characters secrete into their surroundings or the people around them, and which are in the face of death about the savage ambivalence of the human condition, like Samuel Beckett's in *Malone Dies* (1951), whose narrator Malone sets himself an agenda of storytelling between obsessive inventories of his meagre possessions while waiting for death, or to hold off the death of the imagination.⁷ It is no surprise to find that the narrator's grandfather, and also presumably the narrator himself, is called Malone.

If, as has been argued so far, Dabydeen has used elements of a magical worldview to enrich the resources of storytelling as a redemptive form of poesis, the question arises whether these later novels can be categorized as magical realism. Here a brief digression will be necessary to consider how this term is generally understood. Most genealogies trace it back to the 1920s in Paris, and three young Americans who had all been influenced by, but distanced themselves from, surrealism. These were Miguel Ángel Asturias from Guatemala, Alejo Carpentier from Cuba and Arturo Uslar Pietri from Venezuela. Asturias was fascinated by the vanished Maya civilizations, Carpentier by the African elements in Caribbean culture and Pietri by the very cross-culturality of the Caribbean region. It was Pietri who first used the term *realismo mágico* in literary criticism, but Carpentier's formulation was the more significant.[8] According to Tommaso Scarano: "Carpentier's message is quite clear: American reality is a compendium of natural, cultural and historical prodigies, and the unusual, the portentous and the marvellous are components that are typical of American reality. In other words, he proclaims the authentically marvellous character of the real, as opposed to the false marvels of what is unreal" (Scarano 1999, 14). In a lucid and informative essay, "Naturalizing the Supernatural", Christopher Warnes points out that the expression "magical realism" can be found in notes made by the German Romantic poet and philosopher Novalis (Warnes 2005, 2).[9] Warnes goes on to claim that it is possible to distinguish two strands of magical realism, the one represented by Carpentier, founded on faith and a sense that the American real is of a different, marvellous order, while the other, represented by Jorge Luis Borges, depends on an irreverent scepticism born of encyclopaedic reading and a productive sense of marginality. The processes used involve either "naturalizing the marvellous" or "denaturalizing the real". He concludes that "The magic in the magical realist text may have, in postmodern fashion, the effect of unmasking the real, showing up its claims to truth to be provisional and contingent on consensus. Alternatively, the magical may seek to force its way into the company of the real, and thereby to share in the privileged claim the language of realism has to representing the world" (p. 9). As examples, he takes Salman Rushdie's *Satanic Verses* to represent the former, irreverent, approach, while Ben Okri's *The Famished Road* (1991) represents the latter – what Warnes calls faith.

Dabydeen, it seems to me, is really doing both. His playfulness and the multiple perspectives he employs suggest irreverence and the deconstruction of mundane reality, but the Harrisian elements of profundity suggest faith and the reality of enchantment. There is a much older foundation for this than Warnes suggests, the Gnostic/Hermetic tradition mentioned above, with which Novalis and the other Romantics as well as Goethe and Blake were familiar. Blake's poems, it will be recalled, form part of Father Harris's library, and his mysterious writings were the result of his "fourfold" vision, opposed to the Urizenic disenchantment which he described as the reality of Newton's "single vision".[10] In *Der goldene Topf* (1814), E.T.A. Hoffmann, an admirer of

Novalis's work, presents unforgettable images of the realist and realist magical world playfully confronted, when the student Anselmus is talking to some youths on the Elbe bridge in Dresden who are unaware that they are actually, like him, captured in glass jars in a laboratory.

In *Molly and the Muslim Stick* the magical elements have a clearer profile, highlighting the novel's central theme of causality and guilt. An interesting comparison could be made with a contemporaneous work, Hilary Mantel's *Beyond Black* (2005), which also centres on clairvoyance and child abuse in a desolate urban environment. In a world with realist principles, albeit with magical elements, causality determines responsibility for actions and thus guilt. Dabydeen's story begins with Molly's rape by her father, bathed in angelic or demonic light, but this is juxtaposed with the story of Molly as a little girl throwing a stone at a cat to stop it catching a bird: "And what was it all for, the shrieking of the innocent bird, the growling, then the yelping, of the innocent cat? And who was I, the child in their midst, with sorrow for the bird and a spiteful applestone for the cat which travelled through the air and stopped at its skull? Stone. Air. Skull. Death. Why?" (Dabydeen 2008, 4). The same questioning of the origins of guilt in causality drives Om, a creature who is everything and nothing, and thus an angelic figure like Enoch, from the Guiana rainforest to Coventry, where he chances to find Molly. Om had killed a missionary:

> It was not murder. People here don't know how to murder. One day Om picked up a stone and flung it at the man's head. As simple as that: a stone travelled through air and stopped at his skull. Result: death. Stone, air, skull, death. Om didn't understand it, no one did, but all knew that something original had happened in their midst. Think of when the wise men first bent over the crib and caught sight of Christ – the same awe and anguish. (p. 167)

The echoes of T.S. Eliot's "Journey of the Magi", which they were tempted to believe was "all folly", are part of the allusive fabric of this text.

Outside the logic of realism, where instead it is possible for Molly to have necromantic power over Terence and Corinne; where the dead banker and abuser Harold can materialize spewing money or sitting on an aircraft wing; or where a stick begins to talk, reveals it is a Muslim, can translate foreign languages and experiences a full range of human emotions, the reader is subject to a real world of magic. Instead of causality, the logic of the Weird Sisters in Shakespeare's *Macbeth* applies, dependent on puns and wordplay, where "Fair is foul, and foul is fair". The basis of the real, in this case, is not the causally determined material world of traditional realism, but the connections by meaning described by C.G. Jung in his essay on synchronicity. What Jung postulates is the necessity of a "new conceptual language": "Just as the introduction of time as the fourth dimension in modern physics postulates an irrepresentable space-time continuum, so the idea of synchronicity with its inherent quality of meaning produces a picture of the world so irrepresentable as to be completely baffling. The advantage, however, of adding this concept is that it makes possible a view which includes the psychoid factor in our description and knowledge of nature – that is, an a priori meaning or 'equivalence' " (Jung 1969, 513).

This form of representation, dependent on the perceptions of reader and author as well as related events, could be called realist magicalism rather than magical realism. In speaking of the process of artistic creation in an essay on surrealism, but in a way that could apply equally to realist magicalism, Walter Benjamin links occult experiences with artistic and intellectual work: "We penetrate the mystery only to the degree that we recognize it in the everyday world, by virtue of a dialectical optic that perceives the everyday as impenetrable, the impenetrable as everyday" (quoted in Hirsh 2002, 150). If no reliance can be placed on causality, the attempt to seek justice in compensation or retribution is doomed to failure. We are forced to resort to fictions in order to make sense of the world.

When Stick begins to speak, Molly's words resonate with Shakespearean echoes: " 'Oh my Puck and my delight, I'll free your spirit soon,' I interrupted, filled with gratitude and yet guilt for I had neither heeded its voice nor sought its counsel before. 'I have taken insufficient care of thee, pet, but you must forgive me, for I am foolish as you say, though not yet fourscore in age' " (Dabydeen 2008, 71). If Molly speaks in the voice of Lear, from the depths of an experience of becoming nothing, Stick is the spirit Ariel, the enabler of magic. The allusion to Shakespeare is a further sign of the playful seriousness of Dabydeen's project. That Stick is Muslim may on the one hand be taken as a typical Dabydeen provocation in the climate of a "clash of civilisations", but it also recalls the important contribution made by Islam to the Renaissance in Europe and to the preservation of alchemical and hermetic knowledge, and thus to a way of reading texts and experience which Dabydeen's latest fiction exemplifies.

Notes

1. In many Gnostic texts the material universe, created by the Demiurge, is described as an abortion. It is the task of human beings to free themselves from it and pursue the spark of the true God within themselves.
2. This is an example of Dabydeen's playful irreverence coupled with a serious message.
3. I have traced the genealogy of what I term a Gnostic/Hermetic tradition of thought privileging the human imagination in my book *Hidden Mutualities: Faustian Themes from Gnostic Origins to the Postcolonial* (Amsterdam and New York: Rodopi, 2006). Dabydeen is familiar with this work and its bibliography.
4. In the Book of Genesis it merely states "And Enoch walked with God: and he was not; for God took him" (5:24). The literature relating to Enoch and his transformation into the angel Metatron is mainly derived from gnostic Jewish and Islamic sources. It should be noted here that in a recent interview ("The Loose-Tongued Ambassador" in the *Guardian*, 1 April 2008) Dabydeen spoke of being driven to achieve because he saw no immigrants at that time who were the intellectual equals of Enoch Powell.
5. Hirsch is here summarizing Harold Bloom's opinions from *Omens of the Millennium*.
6. One might recall Samuel Beckett's "One of the thieves was saved".
7. Malone's stories of Saposcat, subsequently renamed Macmann, the Lamberts, Moll and Lemuel continue Beckett's search, formidably presented in *Waiting for Godot* and culminating in *Imagination Dead Imagine*, to use the imagination in a real world whose absurdity seems to have undermined the basis of the imagination itself. This is a theme referred to by Wilson Harris in his essay "Imagination Dead Imagine: Bridging a Chasm" (*Yale Journal of Criticism* 7, no. 1 [1994]: 185–95) and in his novel *Jonestown* (1996).
8. I am here omitting the use of the term by Franz Roh in the visual arts, which may have prompted the discussion in the first place. His use corresponds to denaturalizing the real.
9. Warnes includes a brief review of recent scholarship in the field, including the seminal work done by Wendy B. Faris and Lois Parkinson Zamora.
10. For example, Blake's letter to Thomas Butts of 22 November 1822. Of course, we now know that Newton and his "vision" were actually far more complex than Blake could have guessed.

References

Beckett, S. 1958. *Malone Dies*. London: John Calder.

Benjamin, W. 2002. "Surrealism: The Last Snapshot of the European Intelligentsia". In *Reflections: Essays, Aphorisms, Autobiographical Writings*, ed. Peter Demetz, 177–92 (New York: Harcourt Brace Janovich, 1978), quoted in Hirsch, *The Demon and the Angel*.

Dabydeen, D. 2000. "On Samaroo's *Tempus Est*: The Earliest Colonial Rewriting of Shakespeare's *The Tempest*". Talk given at the Royal Festival Hall, London, 8 November 2000, and broadcast on BBC Radio 3, 11 November 2000. *EnterText* 1, no. 1: http://arts.brunel.ac.uk/gate/entertext/et1_In.htm.

———. 2004. *Our Lady of Demerara*. Chichester: Dido Press.

———. 2006. "The Painterboy of Demerara". *Arts Journal* 2, no. 2. Reprinted in *Avocado* (July 2007): 3.

———. 2008. *Molly and the Muslim Stick*. Oxford: Macmillan Caribbean.

Davey, K. 2004. "Black Writing: Traditional Past, Bold Future". *Tribune* Books. 3 December, 22.

Harris, W. 1983. "Harlequin and Psyche". In *The Womb of Space: The Cross-Cultural Imagination*. Westport, CT: Greenwood Press.

Hirsch, E. 2002. *The Demon and the Angel: Searching for the Source of Artistic Inspiration*. New York: Harcourt.

Jung, C.G. 1969. "Synchronicity: An Acausal Connecting Principle". In *The Collected Works*, vol. 8. London: Routledge and Kegan Paul.

Scarano, T. 1999. "Spanish-American Magical Realism". In *Coterminous Worlds: Magical Realism and Contemporary Post-Colonial Literature in English*, ed. E. Linguanti, F. Casotti, and C. Concilio, 9–28. Amsterdam and Atlanta: Rodopi.

Valere, C.D. 2008. Review of *Molly and the Muslim Stick*. *Signifyin' Guyana*: http://signifyinguyana.typepad.com/signifyin_guyana/2008/12/a-guyanacaribbeanfocused-review-of-david-dabydeens-molly-and-the-muslim-stick.html.

Warnes, C. 2005. "Naturalizing the Supernatural: Faith, Irreverence and Magical Realism". *Literature Compass* 2: 1–16.

Williams, W. (N.D. Williams) 2009. Review of *Molly and the Muslim Stick*. *Guyana Caribbean Politics*: http://www.guyanacaribbeanpolitics.com/books/muslim_stick.html.

Contributors

LYNNE MACEDO is Associate Fellow of the Centre for Caribbean Studies at the University of Warwick and (joint) general editor of the Guyana Classics Library. She is the author of a monograph: *Fiction and Film: The Influence of Cinema on Writers from Jamaica and Trinidad*, co-editor of *No Land, No Mother: Essays on David Dabydeen* and editor of *Pak's Britannica: Articles and Interviews with David Dabydeen*. She has published several articles on the Caribbean and is a contributor to the *Oxford Companion to Black British History* and *Blackwell's Encyclopaedia of Twentieth-Century Fiction*.

JENNY DE SALVO is a teacher of Italian as a second language for adult migrants. She has previously published translations of English contemporary poetry, and is currently working on an Italian translation of David Dabydeen's *The Intended*.

ERIK FALK is a lecturer in English at Södertörn University, Sweden.

MONICA MANOLACHI is a PhD candidate at the University of Bucharest, Romania, and a former research associate at Oxford Brookes University. She has taught English language and culture at the University of Bucharest and at International House Bucharest.

NICOLE MATOS is Assistant Professor of English at the College of DuPage in Glen Ellyn, Illinois.

MICHAEL MITCHELL is Associate Fellow of the Centre for Caribbean Studies at the University of Warwick. He is the author of *Hidden Mutualities: Faustian Themes from Gnostic Origins to the Postcolonial*.

ANJALI NERLEKAR is Assistant Professor, Department for African, Middle Eastern and South Asian Languages and Literatures, Rutgers University, New

Jersey. She has previously taught in India and Bahrain and is currently working on a book on bilingualism, translation and Indian poetry.

JUTTA SCHAMP is a lecturer at California State University, Dominguez Hills; California State University, Northridge; and Santa Monica College. She is the author of *Die Repräsentation von Zeit in Shakespeares* Richard II, Henry IV *und* Macbeth (*The Representation of Time in Shakespeare's* Richard II, Henry IV *and* Macbeth).

LILIANA SIKORSKA is the author of numerous books on medieval and contemporary literature, including *A Short History of English Literature*; editor of a number of books on contemporary literature in English, including *Aspects of Suffering: Classical Themes in Literature in English* and *A Universe of (Hi)Stories: Essays on J.M. Coetzee*; and editor of the journal *Studies in Literature in English*.

ABIGAIL WARD is Senior Lecturer in Postcolonial Studies, Nottingham Trent University. She is the author of *Caryl Phillips, David Dabydeen and Fred D'Aguiar: Representations of Slavery*.

RUSSELL WEST-PAVLOV is Professor of English, University of Pretoria, South Africa. His recent books include *Spaces of Fiction/Fictions of Space: Postcolonial Place and Literary DeiXis* and *North-South/East-West: Global Entanglements in Post-Imperial Writing in French and German*.

CPSIA information can be obtained at www.ICGtesting.com
Printed in the USA
BVOW080927290313

316812BV00001B/37/P